A Study of

English Romanticism

NORTHROP FRYE

A Study of

English Romanticism

The University of Chicago Press

The University of Chicago Press, Chicago 60637
The Harvester Press Limited, Brighton, Sussex

Phoenix edition 1982
Printed in the United States of America

89 88 87 86 85 84 83 82   1 2 3 4 5

Library of Congress Cataloging in Publication Data

Frye, Northrop.
    A study of English romanticism.

    Reprint. Originally published: New York: Random House,
1968. (Studies in language and literature; SLL 21)
    Includes bibliographical references.
    1. English poetry—19th century—History and criticism.
2. Romanticism—England. 3. Beddoes, Thomas Lovell,
1803–1849. Death's jest-book. 4. Shelley, Percy Bysshe,
1792–1822. Prometheus unbound. 5. Keats, John, 1795–
1821. Endymion. I. Title. II. Series: Studies in language and
literature (Random House); SLL 21.
PR571.F79   1982   820'.9'145   82-11018
ISBN 0-226-26651-6

Preface

This book is an attempt to introduce the reader to the conception of "Romanticism," more particularly as found in English literature. The first chapter grows out of an earlier essay, to be found in *Romanticism Reconsidered* (1963), which treated the Romantic movement as primarily a change in the language of poetic mythology, brought about by various historical and cultural forces. This thesis is then illustrated by critical discussions of three major works of Romantic English literature: Beddoes' *Death's Jest-Book*, Shelley's *Prometheus Unbound*, and Keats' *Endymion*. Any reader who finds the approach to these poets somewhat peripheral is asked to remember that this is not a book on Beddoes or Keats or Shelley, but a book on Romanticism as illustrated by some of their works. There is a good deal of excellent and central criticism available on the major Romantic poets, and the present book makes no effort to compete with it, much less replace any of it.

The essays on the three poems have grown out of a series of public lectures delivered to the Graduate School of Western Reserve University in May 1966. I am much indebted to my hosts there for stimulating discussions and criticisms. I am also indebted to the Canada Council for a grant which enabled me to work on this and other projects.

N. F.

Toronto, 1967

Contents

PREFACE   *v*

The Romantic Myth   *3*

YORICK: *The Romantic Macabre*   *51*

PROMETHEUS: *The Romantic Revolutionary*   *87*

ENDYMION: *The Romantic Epiphanic*   *125*

NOTES   *167*

BIBLIOGRAPHY   *171*

INDEX   *175*

A Study of

English Romanticism

The Romantic Myth

The word Romanticism is a cultural term, and partly a historical one as well. Historically, it refers to the literature, and in lesser degree the painting, music, and some of the philosophy, produced in the period c. 1780–1830, the period of the French Revolution, the Napoleonic wars, and the nationalistic movements in Greece, Italy, and Germany that followed. It is not however purely a historical term like "medieval," for within the Romantic period we feel that some artists are Romantics and that others are not, or are much less so. The further we move from the arts, the less sure we are of the importance of the term. If we were studying the history of science, the notion of a Romantic movement would hardly occur to us, even though we can see some parallel developments in the science of the time when we compare it with other aspects of culture. The implication seems to be that, for the literary critic at least, the word Romanticism refers primarily to some kind of change in the structure of literature itself, rather than to a change in beliefs, ideas, or political movements reflected in literature. We begin by studying Romanticism on the level of vogue or fashion, which can be characterized only vaguely: literature becomes less rational and more emotional, less urbanized and with more feeling for nature, less witty and more oracular, and so on. But as these formulations gradually cease to satisfy us, we are driven to more and more central reconsiderations about the nature of literature to account for what is, after all, a genuine fact of literary experience: the feeling that a new kind of sensibility comes into all Western literatures around the later part of the eighteenth century.

The informing structures of literature are myths, that is, fictions and metaphors that identify aspects of human personality with the natural environment, such as stories about sun-gods or tree-gods. The metaphorical nature of the god who is both a person and a class of natural objects makes myth, rather than folktale or legend, the direct ancestor of literature. It also gives to myth, in primitive cultures, a particular importance in establishing a society's views of its own origin, including the reasons for its divisions into different classes or groups, its legal sanctions, and its prescribed rituals. The canonical significance which distinguishes the myth from less important fictions also causes myths to form large unified structures, or mythologies, which tend to become encyclopedic in extent, covering all aspects of a society's vision of its situation and destiny. As civilization develops, mythology divides into two main aspects. Its patterns of stories and images, attracting and absorbing those of legend and folktale, become the fictions and metaphors of literature. At the same time, there are also germs of conceptual ideas in myths which extend into theology, philosophy, political theory, and, in earlier ages, science, and become informing principles there as well.

There are thus two structures in a culture which descend from mythology: one is literature, which inherits the fictional and metaphorical patterns of mythology, and the other is a body of integrating or cohering ideas, also mainly fictional, in religion, philosophy, and kindred disciplines. At any given period of literature the conventions of literature are enclosed within a total mythological structure, which may not be explicitly known to anyone, but is nevertheless present as a shaping principle. In every age, the most ambitious literary structures, such as the works of Dante, Milton, Victor Hugo, or Joyce, tend to become cosmological, and hence nearest to suggesting what the total structure is like. Such cosmological works have conceptual forms analogous to and roughly contemporary with them: thus Dante's *Commedia* has a conceptual analogy in the *summa* form of St. Thomas. In Western Europe an encyclopedic myth, derived mainly from the Bible, dominated both the literary and the philosophical traditions for centuries. I see Romanticism as the beginning of the first major change in this pattern of mythology, and as fully comprehensible only when seen as such.

The starting point of most mythologies is a creation myth, the story of how things came to be. This myth has normally two parts, a cosmological myth of the origin of the world, and a proto-historical myth of the origin of man. It is probable that the earliest creation myths were sexual and cyclical in shape, assuming that man and the world simply came into existence in the same way that babies are born and seeds grow in spring. The etymology of the Latin *natura* and the Greek *physis* connects them with ideas of growing and being born. Such myths tend to become mother-centered myths, where nature is an earth-goddess renewing her vitality (in more sophisticated versions her virginity) every spring. If the role of the male in conception is understood, the earth-goddess may be thought of as impregnated by sun or wind or rain, or she may be attended by a subordinate male figure who is successively her son, her lover, and eventually her sacrificial victim. The mother-goddess seems to be morally a most ambiguous figure, who, depending on her phase, may be anything from the blushing bride of the Song of Songs to the ferocious Cybele of Catullus' Attis Ode.

We can only guess about these ancient myths from their vestiges in historical times. The mother-centered myth has always been attractive to poets, and the creation stories of Ovid and Lucretius owe a great deal to it. But the more aggressive myths of Judaism, Christianity, and Plato's *Timaeus* reflect an urban, tool-using, male-dominated society, where the central figure usually develops out of a father-god associated with the sky. Poets, said Horace, are born and not made: Bernard Shaw remarks that that is a rather silly thing to say, in view of the fact that everybody is born and not made. But not according to the most influential of the mythological structures which have controlled our thinking from the dawn of history to the middle of the eighteenth century. This mythology said that the world was made, as an artefact or creature, by a divine artisan or demiurge; and that whatever may be true of men and women now, the first man and the first woman were also made, as watches and tables and pictures are made. The alternation of chicken and egg has to stop somewhere, and

Christianity, along with most other religions and philosophies, stopped it firmly with the chicken.

In the centuries preceding Romanticism, especially during the Middle Ages, the mythology that begins with this artificial creation myth reached its highest point of development. According to it, man and nature were both creatures of God: there are no gods in nature, and what man should look at nature for is the evidence for the intelligent design in its creation that it presents. This attitude naturally gave central prominence to the subject-object relationship, and stressed the rational in contrast to the empirical attitude to nature. The subject-object relation is most marked, and the sense of design clearest, in the study of the stars. The movements of the stars were, so to speak, the diagram of the universe as a created order, and astronomy was the one science that a learned medieval poet, such as Dante or Chaucer, would naturally be assumed to know. Dante's Paradiso is symbolized by the heavenly bodies, and the starry spheres, with their unheard harmonies, form the central image of nature as God had originally designed it, before the lower part of it "fell" with man into an unsymmetrical chaos. God's work in nature was most clearly revealed in what Sir Thomas Browne calls "the mystical mathematics of the City of Heaven," and except in the most refined and sophisticated aspects of philosophy, his connection with the sky was considerably more than a poetic metaphor.

Occasionally one glimpses what may be traces of an older matriarchal mythology, partly outlawed and partly absorbed into its successor. Christianity replaced the earth-goddess and her dying god with a Queen of Heaven receiving her crown from the son whom she had nursed and whose death she had lamented. Nietzsche's formula "Dionysus versus Christ" is present in institutional Christianity too, in reverse. The enemies of Christ and his mother are the devil and his dam: the devil has the horns and hoofs of a woodland god, and his dam is incarnate in the witch who worships him. The theory that a cult of a "horned god" identified with the devil actually existed in the Middle Ages is difficult to swallow, but that the symbolic outlines of a "Satanic" perversion of Christianity could be extracted from suspected witches by torture, in an insane parody of psychoanalysis, is obvious enough. In the miracle plays about the flood, Noah's wife is often recalcitrant and un- willing to enter the ark, perhaps recalling an earlier version of the story in which the ark, the container of all life, was her body and not his artefact. But in general there was little opposition to the principle that there were no gods, or goddesses either, in nature, and that if man looked to find deities there they would turn into devils.

Man should see nature, the myth said, with his reason as the work of God. If he attempted to approach it differently, in search of mysterious power or the sense of the numinous, he found powerful forces pulling him in the opposite direc- tion, toward his own reason and his own society. He found that he was a moral being capable of sin, and could not imitate the innocence of animals. Christianity explained this by saying that his nature was originally designed by God to be something essentially different from animal na- ture, and that his present natural context was a "fallen" one. Identification with the forces and powers of nature is a tendency that Christianity regarded as pagan, the effective pagan gods, from this point of view, being Eros and Diony- sus, sexuality and emotional abandon. To regain his true identity man had to keep the barrier of consciousness against nature, and think of himself first as a social being. The supreme symbol of the distinction between human nature and physical nature was the city, along with the constituent or supporting images of the city, such as the court, the cathedral, the highway, the castle. Heaven, the place of the divine presence, is a habitation, a city of God. However, if man could completely recover his lost identity as a child of God, through the social disciplines of law, morality, and religion, he would also find a renewed identity with nature, back in the garden in which God had originally put him, the garden being the symbol of nature made over in the image of conscious man. This wistful longing for a reintegration with nature is what is expressed in literature by the pastoral, the vision of a simplified rural shepherd's life where art and love-making have recovered some of their lost spontaneity and innocence.

Outside the pastoral, and even often within it, images of plants and animals tended to be stylized and heraldic, serving for religious emblems, moral lessons, mythological allusions, and social metaphors. The poets knew, of course, much better than the theologians and philosophers, how powerful the "pagan" forces of nature were. The poets in fact reincorporated the pagan deities into their poetry and developed an elaborate mock-theology around the god Eros, in which a morally ambiguous goddess-figure, at once adorable and sinister, reappears. But this was understood to have its own subordinate place in the scheme of things, the controlling framework being one of stability and harmony. Man was subject to moral law, nature to natural law; the two forms of law had one source in the will of God, and the circling of the stars symbolized the perfection of obedience which would be man's perfect freedom. The universe of this myth was a projection of man's own body: the rational design was visible on top, just as the reason is on top of the human body, and the two were connected by the sense of distance, the eye. The erotic and Dionysian world was much lower down, always potentially subversive, always apt to get above itself and seek less rational forms of communion.

Poetry attempts to unite nature with man by the primitive and simple forms of union, analogy and identity, simile and metaphor. In doing so it shows its affinity with and descent from the myth, the story about a god, who, we said, as sun-god or sea-god or what not, identifies a personality and an aspect of nature. The Christian myth told the story of how there was once an identity of God, man, and nature, how man fell from God and broke the harmony with nature, and how man is to be reintegrated. In its fully developed form this myth was, down to the seventeenth century, comprehensive enough to unite the theologian and the philosopher with the poet and the scientist. The poet, on the whole, accepted an attitude to the world which put faith and reason above the response to poetry, but the scientist was in a more difficult position. The attitude to nature as an objective system is congenial enough to the scientist, for whom nature is always the world out there, to be studied by the rational consciousness. At the same time, the scientist was working within a mythological construct which had been founded on identity and analogy, on correspondences and simple symmetries. His sciences, in short, were full of myths, in which astronomy and chemistry had not yet been completely separated from astrology and alchemy. To the scientist, myth is simply illusion: or perhaps one should say that science creates its own mythology. Sooner or later, as science developed, it was bound to break loose from the mythological construct. And in proportion as it took on its own form, it forced poets to look for another construct, and, in doing so, to realize that all myths are poetic in origin.

For example: we said that for the sense of nature as a

created order the primary images were those of the heavenly bodies, all that is now left of nature as God had originally designed it. But from the point of view of science, such imagery rested on illusion, the illusion of a geocentric universe, of planets revolving in symmetrical spheres, probably guided by angels, of mysterious correspondences of the seven planets with the seven metals and seven aspects of human temperament. When the new science of Copernicus and Galileo began to make its impact, this illusion became more and more of a historical relic. Newton spiced his scientific and mathematical findings with philosophical and religious speculations which aroused great enthusiasm at the time. But the enthusiasm was temporary and the poetry it inspired mediocre. The old feeling of heaven, in the sense of the sky, as an image of heaven in the sense of the place of the presence of God, was undeniably going, and could never return in quite the same form. The more man learned about the heavenly bodies, the less emotionally convinced he could be that they were different in kind from the sublunary nature he was more familiar with. They were not made out of quintessence, but out of the same elements as the lower world; they did not move in perfect circles or symbolize an immortal purity from corruption. The sky seemed just as indifferent to human concerns, just as permeated with mindless law, as the least conscious part of the earth. An apocalyptic vision of a day when the sun would be turned into darkness and the moon into blood had to give place to a science which turned the sun into a blast furnace and the moon into a stone. The crystal spheres of Milton's *Nativity Ode,* making up full consort with the angelic symphony, eventually become Thomas Hardy's

> *Mountains of magnitude without a shape,*
> *Hanging amid deep wells of nothingness.*

Much more is involved here than merely the loss of a traditional poetic metaphor. Poets are dependent on images, and the image of the order and harmony of the "up there" was the guarantee of the order and harmony of the "out there," the sense of nature as a structure or system, a vertical chain of being, looked at by the rational and conscious subject. Once the heavenly bodies come to be seen as a dead and mechanical part of creation, the highest aspect of nature that man can perceive becomes the living part of it, the world of organisms, of animals and plants, and of man so far as man is an organic and vital being. One's relationship to the rest of life then becomes a participating relationship, an identity of process rather than a separation of subjective and objective creatures or products.

When we start reading Wordsworth and Coleridge we are struck with the way in which the old subject-object relationship has been demoted. The reason founded on a separation of consciousness from nature is becoming an inferior faculty of the consciousness, more analytic and less constructive, the outside of the mind dealing with the outside of nature; determined by its field of operation, not free; descriptive, not creative. The artist, the Aristotelian tradition had said, imitates nature: this means, according to Coleridge, not that he studies the *natura naturata,* the world out there, like the scientist, but that he "imitates" the *natura naturans* or living process of nature by seeking a union of himself, as a living and creating being, with nature as process or genesis. Here physical nature becomes symbolically related to human nature; as Beddoes says:

> *Thus it is with man;*
> *He looks on nature as his supplement,*
> *And still will find out likenesses and tokens*

> *Of consanguinity, in the world's graces,*
> *To his own being.*

Of all the great English Romantic poets, William Blake was the one who grasped the implications of this change in mythology most completely. For Blake, the God who created the natural order is a projected God, an idol constructed out of the sky and reflecting its mindless mechanism. Such a God is a figment of man's alienation, for the tyranny of an absurd and meaningless nature suggests and guarantees the tyranny of exploiting ruling classes. Thus the projected sky-god is really Satan, the accuser of man and the prince of the power of the air. The true God is Jesus, who is identified with struggling and suffering humanity. In *Europe* (1794) Blake shows how the tyranny of the Roman Empire, backed by the mysterious hierarchy of star-gods, was threatened by the Incarnation, how eighteen centuries of institutional Christianity had managed to contain the threat, and how, after Newton had blown the last trumpet for its mythology, revolution had begun again in "the vineyards of red France."

Similarly Shelley argues for the "necessity of atheism," and urges in his notes to *Queen Mab* that "all that miserable tale of the Devil, and Eve, and an Intercessor, with the childish mummeries of the God of the Jews, is irreconcilable with the knowledge of the stars." Whatever one thinks of this argument, Shelley is right in maintaining that the miserable tale is not an integral part of the modern science of astronomy, as it is, for example, of the astronomical speculations of Dante's *Convivio*. At the same time "the hypothesis of a pervading spirit co-eternal with the universe" remains unaltered for Shelley. That is, God, if he exists at all, can exist only as existence, as an aspect of our own identity, and not as a hypothesis attached to the natural order. In *Prometheus Unbound* Jupiter is a projected sky-god of the same type as the sky-gods in Blake, Urizen, Nobodaddy, and Satan. In Byron's *Vision of Judgement* and the Prologue to Goethe's *Faust* the traditional conception of God as a miraculous juggler of planets is only a subject for parody.

We are now in a position to see that one central element of this new mythological construction is a recovery of projection. In the older myth, God was ultimately the only active agent. God had not only created the world and man: he had also created the forms of human civilization. The traditional images of civilization are the city and the garden: the models of both were established by God before Adam was created. Law, moral principles, and, of course, the myth itself were not invented by man, but were part of God's revelation to him. Gradually at first, in such relatively isolated thinkers as Vico, then more confidently, the conviction grows that a great deal of all this creative activity ascribed to God is projected from man, that man has created the forms of his civilization, including his laws and his myths, and that consequently they exhibit human imperfections and are subject to human criticism. For Hooker in Elizabethan times, law had its origin in the divine mind: the perfection of natural law was a part of it, and obedience to laws of church and state followed deductively from certain mythical premises like "natural right." In the Romantic period an iconoclastic development of legal reform took place (although very little of it was carried out by people that we think of as Romantics), and the assumption of this reform was that such mythical premises were mostly rationalizations of class privilege. Again, liberty, for Shelley, is what man wants and what the gods he invents out of cowardice and superstition oppose his getting. But in the pre-Romantic period, even for the revolutionary Milton, liberty is what God wants for man, and not anything that man naturally wants for himself.

Romanticism, thus considered, is the first major phase in an imaginative revolution which has carried on until our own day, and has by no means completed itself yet. (It may look from my account as though it would be complete when everything formerly ascribed to God has been transferred to man or nature, but that would in my opinion be far too simple a solution.) This means that everything that has followed Romanticism, including the anti-Romantic movements in France and England of fifty to sixty years ago, is best understood as post-Romantic. Many aspects of Romanticism become much more clearly understood if we look forward to what later writers did with them. In particular, I find that the major works of Joyce, Eliot, Proust, Yeats, and D. H. Lawrence provide essential clues to the nature of literary trends and themes that began with the Romantics. Then again, many Romantic writers, both philosophical and literary, were deeply interested in contemporary science, and made heroic efforts to unify the humanistic and scientific perspectives, usually on some basis of a philosophy of organism. In English literature, the social sciences had as much if not more prestige than the physical sciences, De Quincey's enthusiasm for Ricardo being as typical in its way as Goethe's interest in color perception and comparative anatomy. But with the hindsight of another century and a half, one century of which has been after Darwin, we can see that the scientific vision of nature was inexorably splitting away from the poetic and existential vision of Romantic mythology. Every generation since then has produced a cosmology attempting to unite the two again (Teilhard de Chardin is the leading example at present), but cosmologies have a high rate of mortality, and in any case are usually founded, not directly on scientific principles, but on mythological analogies to scientific principles.

The separating of science from what we may call the myth of concern, society's view of its situation and destiny, has another important consequence. Romanticism is a new mythology, but society uses its mythology in different ways. The Christian mythology of the Middle Ages and later was a closed mythology, that is, a structure of belief, imposed by compulsion on everyone. As a structure of belief, the primary means of understanding it was rational and conceptual, and no poet, outside the Bible, was accorded the kind of authority that was given to the theologian. Romanticism, besides being a new mythology, also marks the beginning of an "open" attitude to mythology on the part of society, making mythology a structure of imagination, out of which beliefs come, rather than directly one of compulsory belief. Beliefs for a long time continued much as they had been held, except that the Romantic expression of belief in, say, traditional Christianity often becomes vaguer and more purely rhetorical in statement. At the same time, the new mythology caused old things to be believed in a new way, and thus eventually transformed the spirit of their belief. It also made new types of belief possible, by creating a new mythical language that permitted their formulation. Of these, two are of particular importance for the present argument.

One is the revived sense of the numinous power of nature, as symbolized in Eros, Dionysus, and Mother Nature herself. With the Romantic movement there comes a return to something very like a polytheistic imagination. The avenging spirit of the Ancient Mariner is a portent of much to follow: the forsaken Classical gods who haunt so many German Romantics, the spirits of Strindberg and Yeats, the angels of Rilke, the dark gods of Lawrence. All these illustrate the principle which Freud perhaps more than anyone else has made us aware of. When our attention is focused on ourselves and our existential relation to nature, as distinct from the attention of science which is turned toward natural law and the attention of theology which is turned toward an intelligent personal God, we become immediately conscious of a plurality of conflicting powers. The second type of new belief comes from the ability that Romantic mythology conferred of being able to express a *revolutionary* attitude toward society, religion, and personal life. We shall return to this in a moment.

In the older mythology the myth of creation is followed by a gigantic cyclical myth, outlined in the Bible, which begins with the fall of man, is followed by a symbolic vision of human history, under the names of Adam and Israel, and ends with the redemption of Adam and Israel by Christ. The two poles are the alienation myth of fall, the separation of man from God by sin, and the reconciling, identifying, or atoning myth of redemption which restores to man his forfeited inheritance. Translated into Romantic terms, this myth assumes a quite different shape. What corresponds to the older myth of an unfallen state, or lost paradise of Eden, is now a sense of an original identity between the individual man and nature which has been lost. It may have been something lost in childhood, as in Wordsworth's *Ode on Intimations of Immortality,* or it may be something hazier like a racial or collective memory, but it haunts the mind with the same sense of dispossession that the original Eden myth did.

The context of what corresponds to the "fall," or the myth of alienation, changes accordingly. Man has "fallen," not so much into sin as into the original sin of self-consciousness, into his present subject-object relation to nature, where, because his consciousness is what separates him from nature, the primary conscious feeling is one of separation. The alienated man cut off from nature by his consciousness is the Romantic equivalent of post-Edenic Adam. He is forcefully presented in Coleridge's figure of the Ancient Mariner, compelled recurrently to tell a story whose moral is reintegration with nature. The Romantic redemption myth then becomes a recovery of the original identity. For the sense of an original unity with nature, which being born as a subjective consciousness has broken, the obvious symbol is the mother. The lost paradise becomes really an unborn world, a pre-existent ideal. As a result something of the ancient mother-centered symbolism comes back into poetry. Wordsworth leaves no doubt that he thinks of nature as Mother Nature, and that he associates her with other maternal images. In the myth of recovery we often have a bride whose descent from a mother-figure is indicated by the fact that, in Shelley, in Byron obliquely, and in Blake's Preludium to *America,* she is frequently a sister as well.

Wordsworth and Coleridge, especially Wordsworth, had, to an extent that they hardly realized themselves, inherited a recent (i.e., eighteenth-century) conception of a "natural society" which, for the first time in many centuries, had raised a central question about human identity. In the older myth, man was morally and intellectually separated from nature, hence his identity was primarily a social one, and the symbol of that social identity was, as said above, the city. In his evolution as a child of God, the city of God came first, then the garden of man as its suburb. Milton thinks of man's original nature in Eden as simple and pastoral but nevertheless civilized; Adam, for Milton, does not become the archetypal noble savage until after his fall. Rousseau had suggested that perhaps the anomalies and injustices of civilization were so great as to make one doubt whether this city-garden order is the right one or not. Perhaps man should seek an identity with nature first, not nature in its humanized form of a garden or park but simply nature as physical environment. After that, the genuine form of human society may have a chance to emerge. The sense of antagonism to the city, as a kind of cancerous growth destroying the relation of man and nature, which later comes out so strongly in Baudelaire's *fourmillante cité,* Eliot's "unreal city" and Verhaeren's *villes tentaculaires,* is already emerging in the London scenes of Wordsworth's *Prelude.* By contrast, it is rude or uncultivated nature, nature "unspoiled" by man and not transformed into a narcissistic image of himself, that comes to be thought of as complementing human nature and completing its being.

In Wordsworth also man first finds his identity in his relation to physical nature, in its rude or uncultivated form. In the older myth there were two levels of nature: an upper level of human nature, represented by the Garden of Eden and the Golden Age, which God had originally intended for man, and a lower level of physical nature, permeated by death, corruption, and, for man at least, sin, which man fell into. According to this construct, man is in the physical world but not of it, and only an elaborate social training, comprising education, law, morality, and religion, can help to raise him toward his proper level. In Wordsworth the existing social and educational structure is artificial, full of inert custom and hypocrisy. Nature is a better teacher than books, and one finds one's lost identity with nature in moments of feeling in which one is penetrated by the sense of nature's "huge and mighty forms." Thus already in Wordsworth it is the "pagan" or latent numinous powers in nature that man turns to. Wordsworth shook his head over the Hymn to Pan in the first book of Keats'

Endymion and called it "a very pretty piece of paganism." But Wordsworth had done much, was probably the decisive influence, in making the Hymn to Pan possible, and Keats in his turn helped to create a new sensibility that ultimately led to the rebirth of Eros and Dionysus in Yeats and D. H. Lawrence.

Similarly, the redemption myth in the older mythology emphasized the free act of God in offering man grace, grace being thought of as essentially the transformation of the human moral will. Such grace proceeded from a divine love or *agape*. Romantic redemption myths, especially the revolutionary ones like those of Shelley, throw the emphasis on an *eros,* or love rooted in the human sexual instinct. Such an *eros* develops a distinctively human idealism, and for such idealism the redeeming agent is also human-centered. The *agape* or love of God for man creates grace, but what man's love and idealism create is essentially a gnosis, an expanded knowledge or consciousness, and one that is more inclusive and profound than the conscious knowledge of the detached subject. This greater gnosis is identified with the imagination in Wordsworth's *Prelude* and in Coleridge: it is often, as in Coleridge, considered to be a superior kind of reason; it is explicitly identified with love (in the sense of *eros,* of course) in Shelley; in many French and German Romantics it acquires a quasi-occult or theosophical cast; in some, such as Novalis, it could be called a mystical consciousness. In the more conservative and nostalgic it is apt to become simply an overwhelming of the reason with mysteries that only faith, thought of as an intuitive or nonanalytic mode of consciousness, can reach. In any case it is the power both of creation and of response to creation, just as the reason is equally the power which can construct or follow a rational argument.

This transposition of the traditional myth makes for a

considerable change in the poet's view of his social function. Earlier poets and critics had been well aware of the "creative" nature of the arts and of the poet's role in articulating society, or being what Shelley calls an unacknowledged legislator. But if nature was, to quote Sir Thomas Browne again, the art of God, the human artist could hardly compete with nature, and if the myths and moral principles of society were divinely revealed, the primary instrument for understanding them was the reason. The fulfillment of right knowledge is right action, but knowledge by itself does not lead to virtuous action. The bridge is built, in the older mythology, by a careful education in moral and religious behavior, and poetry, rightly used, is one of the instruments of this education. Hence the commonplace among pre-Romantic critics that poetry provides a vivid image, or speaking picture, a kind of controlled hallucination, of virtue and of its opposite vice, which persuades the emotions as well as the intelligence to identify with virtue and repudiate vice. The poet is thus to be judged rhetorically, by his skill in ornamenting or embellishing a certain kind of content in such a way as to help the reader to pass from enlightenment to moral freedom. This freedom is not, of course, a mere moralism: it includes every aspect of civilized life, but then civilized life itself was thought of as essentially moral, in the broad sense. Even Milton thought of his authority as prophetic rather than strictly poetic: he was a great poet and he knew it, but because he knew it he felt responsible for using his genius rightly, that is, allied to certain moral and religious attitudes.

The Romantic conception of the poet had several new and revolutionary aspects. First comes the principle that if man has invented the forms of his own civilization, then the artist becomes the man professionally concerned with developing and shaping those forms, which makes him the central figure in that civilization. Along with this goes the conception of the *serious* writer, the writer who, in contrast to the popular entertainer, does not aim to please but to enlighten and expand the consciousness of his audience. Such a writer would instinctively set his face against most of society, both in his art and in his mode of life. With Romanticism came the conception of artists as forming a *Davidsbündler* out to kill the Goliaths or Philistine giants of the social establishment, a conception which expanded into the later *vie de Bohème* and other expressions of art as not only a social craft but a means of building up a kind of counter-society. There is of course nothing new in the conception of the serious writer as such: what is new is the conception of genius as autonomous, as having an authority of its own apart from its moral context. Blake had a strong sense of the moral responsibility of the poet, and understood very well what Milton meant by "that one talent which is death to hide." But Milton could never have uttered Blake's aphorism: "Genius has no Error." Hence a feature in Romanticism which at first glance seems contradictory. The Romantic poet often feels, even more oppressively than his predecessors, that his calling as a poet is a dedication, a total way of life, and that a commitment to it has an importance for society far beyond poetry itself. Yet it was the Romantic conception of the authority of genius that finally made it possible for criticism to base itself on a purely disinterested aesthetic response to which all moral factors have to be subordinated. Both elements, the sense of dedication to art and of freedom from moral factors in the experience of art, were greatly intensified later in the nineteenth century.

The conception of the autonomy of creative power reinforces the question: is this power a special function of the mind, distinct from reason or memory? This takes us back to the gnosis already referred to, and which is generally called imagination. The question of a special function hardly needed to be raised as long as the poet's work was thought of rhetorically, as a particular kind of expertise with words. But, we have seen, Romantic poets felt that the reason of the detached consciousness was something different from and inferior to the imagination or faculty of bringing poetic forms into existence. Imagination participates with nature as a process, and imitates specifically its power of bringing organisms to birth. In English literature, Shakespeare is the most impressive example of a poet who creates people, societies, even complete worlds, much as nature herself does, and this conception of imagination raised Shakespeare almost to divinity, as the supreme example of its power. The imagination is a "sympathetic" faculty, as Hazlitt called it, allied to love, in contrast to the reason, which is often aggressive and analytical. The Romantics in general did not go so far as to suggest that the conception of God as creator and maker of the world had been projected from the fact that man creates and makes things. What they felt was rather an analogy between God and man as creators, between God's Word and the poet's word, between God's revelation in the Scriptural myth and the poet's revelation, which for most Romantics was also a distinctively mythopoeic revelation.

In the centuries before Romanticism, the poets worked out their imagery within a mythological structure derived from certain organizing conceptions, the chain of being, the Ptolemaic universe, and the like. The historians of science, of philosophy, and of religion will look at this structure in different ways, and for the historian of literature it is different again. It may most conveniently be summarized, for the purposes of literary criticism, as a schema of four levels, the levels being best understood, again within a critical context, as spatial. On the top level is God, and the place of the presence of God, or heaven. The only language that can describe this top level is analogical language, and, as we have seen, the imagery of heavenly bodies was central to the analogy, the most conspicuous example being Dante's *Paradiso*. A medieval poet would not necessarily use such imagery in direct relation to God: Chaucer, for instance, often makes it symbolize a malignant fate, as in the star-crossed love of Troilus and in the address to the *primum mobile* in *The Man of Law's Tale*. The malignant influence of the stars does not contradict their divine associations, but constitutes a subordinate aspect of them. In making so functional a use of astronomical imagery, and in seeing in the sky the images of law, purpose, design, the cycle of seasons, and the order of creation, as well as of fate and the source of tragedy, Chaucer is almost closer in mental attitude to the builders of Stonehenge than he is to us.

Next come the two levels of nature, an upper world of human nature, where man was originally intended to live, and a lower world of physical nature, established as man's environment after the fall of Adam. The upper level is represented by the imagery of the Garden of Eden, the Golden Age, and the City of God. Man is no longer in this world, but everything that is good tends to detach him from physical nature and raise him toward his proper level. We may adopt Blake's terms innocence and experience to describe the two natures. Man fell from innocence into experience: his education, religion, and social discipline help him to recover (at least in part: the process is completed in purgatory) his freedom of will which he lost with his innocence. Below the two levels of nature is the demonic world, or hell. We see that this schema has a moral principle incorporated into it: God is good, hell bad, and the human level of nature better than the physical one. Hence, though any form of imagery can be used in either an idyllic or a sinister context, a great deal of the imagery of literature before Romanticism tended to conventionalize itself along moral lines. Reversals of the convention, such as the use of paradisal imagery in a sinister sense, as in Spenser's Bower of Bliss, are as a rule quite clearly marked as such. Again, the structure is an inherently conservative one, providing no place for revolutionary activity, unless initiated by God.

In the Romantic period this schema becomes profoundly modified. There is of course nothing to stop a Romantic or post-Romantic poet from employing the pre-Romantic structure, and we shall later on be looking at a remarkable example of a Romantic poem written mostly in the older tonality, Keats' *Endymion*. But most Romantic poems give marked evidence of a change of attitude. We can still trace a schema on four levels, and we shall try to outline it, for convenience, but the structure becomes much more ambiguous. In the first place, the tendency to moral conventionalizing disappears: all four levels can be seen either as ideal or as demonic, or as anything between. Secondly, we have traced the process by which the imagery of the sky ceased to have a special kind of significance attached to it, and became simply assimilated to the rest of nature. From Blake on, there is a prevailing tendency to see the machinery of the stars and its demiurge as demonic, because expressed only in a mindless automatism. We meet this for instance in Thomas Hardy's *Dynasts*, where the medieval astronomical imagery of fate and fortune is employed without any sense of an intelligent personal God having a power of veto. The moon, largely because of its traditional associations with "lunacy," enjoys a favored position in the poetry of Laforgue and Yeats, but, again, in an ironic context. Sometimes, of course, the heavenly bodies may retain their older role as witnesses of order, though with a stronger emphasis on their purely symbolic function in inspiring a mood of what Tennyson calls higher pantheism. Sometimes too, as frequently in Shelley and Poe, in Byron's *Cain*, and elsewhere, the poet or hero is carried on a journey through the skies, usually in a "car" or other symbol of technological exuberance, which gives him a new (and occasionally, as in Byron, disastrous) knowledge. Out of this convention comes a good deal of modern "science fiction" with its ambiguous attitude to the mysteries of outer space.

The relation of the two levels of nature, human and physical, is also transformed in Romantic poetry. Let us begin with the world of experience, the social structure we live in. In Romanticism we become aware of an increased self-consciousness in historical perspective and in the sense of tradition. The myth of the fall into self-consciousness is projected into history as well, earlier ages being thought of as more spontaneous, naive, and unspoiled in their relation to nature. The structure of contemporary civilization is thought of more as having *accumulated* a past, as less creative because later in time, and more preoccupied with its past because that past is the source of its very self-consciousness. The conservative Romantics who accept the structure of civilization, as something to be imaginatively trusted, tend to stress the traditional elements in it, such elements as church and aristocracy in particular, and lament their decline or hope for their renewal. The Romantic period was a time when aristocracy was fast losing its essential social functions, though its power and prestige remained for much longer, and nostalgia for a vanishing aristocracy is a large element in Romantic fiction. It comes into the "Gothic" and medieval vogues that are so conspicuous in the period, and the popularity of Scott has much to do with his idealizing of Jacobitism and the feudal loyalties of the Scottish Highlands as against the middle-class Hanoverian society that destroyed them. In this vanishing culture the "last minstrel," or symbol of a decline in the traditional function of poetry, also has a place.

In religion, many Romantics, especially on the Continent, adopted a conservative or traditional Christian position, usually Roman Catholic, and saw in Romanticism a revival of an age of faith, in reaction to the sterile enlightenment of the eighteenth century, when a rational and analytic perspective was thought to have reached an extreme. In British Romanticism, Edmund Burke, with his conception of a continuous social contract and his elegy over the passing of the age of chivalry with the French Revolution, and Carlyle, with his effort to reactivate the aristocracy and his vision of the "organic filaments" of a new religion, represent this conservative tendency, along with the later religious writings of Coleridge. It is still surviving in the historical nostalgia of the early Yeats and in the various mythical constructs which show us Western culture as having steadily declined since the Middle Ages, a historical fall being sometimes associated with a certain phase which the mythologist particularly dislikes, such as the Reformation, the philosophy of Bacon, the secularism of the Renaissance, "usura" (Pound), or "dissociation of sensibility" (Eliot).

On the other hand, of course, civilization may be thought of in revolutionary or Rousseauist terms as corrupt and perverted. This view of it immediately involves its relation to the other order of nature, the "unspoiled" nature which corresponds to, yet contrasts with, the older innocent nature. The more irrational society is, the more readily the reasonable may be associated with the natural; and the more unnatural society is, the more readily physical nature becomes the image of its regeneration. For Rousseau, man has lost the identity with physical nature which is also his own identity as a man, and in consequence his civilization has grown artificial, in a new and pejorative sense of that word, in need of a revolution which will recreate the natural society of liberty and equality. This is of course an extreme formulation, though very influential for that reason, of the central Romantic view of man's "fall," or what corresponds to it, as a fall into a self-consciousness separated from nature.

The feeling that physical nature provides the missing complement to human nature takes many forms. In proportion as the old celestial imagery declined, it was replaced by the "sublime," which included it but gave it a different context. The sublime emphasized a sense of mystery and vagueness, not of order or purpose, coming through uncultivated nature, and addressing the individual or solitary man rather than the community. There is nothing new in this as a principle, but locating the sublime in mountains and oceans and wildernesses, where a solitary traveler confronts it, is relatively new as an emphasis in poetic imagery. Longinus, the main source of the theory of the sublime, had discussed it in a professional rhetorical context which is very different from its eighteenth-century picturesque developments. We may also notice the growth of the cliché (for it becomes that) that the "fancy," nourished on solitude and landscape imagery, may cling to some idea or notion that reason or doctrine rejects, with the corollary that it possesses its own kind of truth independently of the truth founded on the subject-object relationship.

From the sublime develops the sense of nature as oracular, as dropping hints of expanding mysteries into the narrowed rational consciousness. One of the most famous, and certainly one of the most eloquent, expressions of this is Baudelaire's sonnet *Correspondances*, but it is also, of course, the central conception in Wordsworth, and it finds its way into popular Romanticism as well. It accounts for much of the use of superstition in the more sensational brands of Romantic fiction, such as the Gothic novels of the 1790s, with their shivery occult imagery, their emphasis on the sensibilities engendered by solitude and sublime landscape, their paternalistic nostalgic conservatism, and their exploiting of the picturesque (the alienated seen as happy) and the exotic (the unfamiliar seen as pleasurable). Mrs. Radcliffe, it is true, writes from a relentlessly enlightened point of view that first summons up a supernatural mystery and then sandbags it with a rational explanation, but she shows her adherence to the oracular tradition in her sensitive heroines, who follow the general Gothic pattern. We may wonder why any literary convention should have produced these absurd creatures, drizzling like a Scotch mist and fainting at every crisis in the plot; but there is clearly something mediumistic about such females—in fact, if the author's interests are explicitly occult they may be actual mediums, like the heroine of Bulwer Lytton's *A Strange Story*. Their sensibility puts them closer to superior forms of consciousness and perception, which are reflected in their fragile and exquisite appearance and their affinity with trance and tears. Jane Austen, in *Love and Freindship,* recommends that such heroines should go mad rather than faint, as a means of getting more fresh air and exercise. Those who take her advice become the wild women or gypsies of Romantic fiction, like the Meg Merrilies and Madge Wildfire of Scott, who also suggest something of the oracular mysteries of nature.

Just as some Romantics are conservative and others radical in their attitudes to the structure of civilization, so some

Romantics regard Mother Nature as a benevolent teacher and others as a bloodthirsty ogress, like the Indian Kali. The Christian Holy Spirit, who is the source of life but not of death, gives place to the ancient and ambiguous "white goddess" who is both destroyer and preserver, in the phrase of Shelley's *Ode to the West Wind,* which adopts the traditional Christian image of the Holy Spirit, the wind, but transfers it to nature. The interaction of beneficence and savagery in nature is so obvious that no poet can altogether avoid the fact that nature is a moral riddle, and that the more directly it is contemplated, the less easy it is to believe in it as something essentially related to the moral structure of human life. Wordsworth's assertion that the "external world is fitted to the mind" carries less conviction (except for science, which is not what Wordsworth is talking about) than Baudelaire's suggestion of a teasing, unpredictable, and ambivalent relation. But even so, such pre-Romantic symbolism as that of Spenser's allegory of the Castle of Alma or Bunyan's *Holy War,* which depicts the temperate or virtuous soul as a fortress beleaguered by an external environment and resisting it on all fronts, gives place to the feeling that the soul has much to learn from parleying with its traditional enemies.

The paradoxical relation of civilized and rude nature, a relation partly antithetical and partly complementary, is often expressed in Romantic fiction and drama by some variant of the struggle-of-brothers theme. This has several Biblical archetypes—Cain and Abel, Esau and Jacob, Ishmael and Isaac—which become important in its development. In the conventional interpretation of the Bible the figures of the social establishment, Isaac and Jacob, are the accepted ones; with Romanticism, there comes a transfer of sympathy to their exiled brethren. The so-called Byronic hero is often a Romantic version of the natural man, who, like Esau or Ishmael, is an outcast, a solitary much given to communing with untamed nature, and who thus represents the potentially expanding and liberating elements in that nature. He has great energy, often great powers of leadership, and even his vices are dignified enough to have some aesthetic attraction. He is often aristocratic in birth or behavior, with a sense that, like Esau, he is the dispossessed rightful heir—here the theme combines with the sense of nostalgia for a vanished aristocracy. When he is evil, there is often the feeling that, as with Byron's Cain, his evil is comprehensible, that he is not wholly evil any more than society is wholly good, and that even his evil is a force that society has to reckon with. The greatest of all his incarnations in English literature, Emily Brontë's Heathcliff, has in full the sense of a natural man who eludes all moral categories just as nature itself does, and who cannot be simply condemned or accepted. In contrast, the Jacob-figure, the defender of the establishment, often seems unheroic and spoiled by a soft or decadent civilization. It was of course Byron himself who popularized the moral ambiguity of the Byronic hero, both in his poetry and, with his reputation as a wicked and infidel lord, in his life. Childe Harold illustrates, like Scott's last minstrel, the close relation of a distinctive social attitude with a distinctive type of poetic imagination. In Byron the struggle-of-brothers theme goes all the way back, from Cain and Abel to the rivalry of Lucifer, the dispossessed elder son of God, and the younger and more favored Son. Thus of Lara it is said:

> *He stood a stranger in this breathing world,*
> *An erring spirit from another hurl'd.*

In the *Vision of Judgement* Lucifer is an icily polite aristocrat: his rival does not appear, but while the prince of darkness is a gentleman, St. Peter is not quite a gentleman, and his chief is clearly operating a somewhat square and bourgeois establishment, one that finds George III easier to absorb than Wilkes.

In the older structure, human nature was almost invariably thought of as *above* physical nature, in imagery as in value. Eden is usually on a mountain-top, and the structure of civilization and social discipline raises man above the level of physical nature, in imagery as in conceptual metaphor. In Wordsworth physical nature has inherited a good deal of the older conception of the lost state of innocence, hence it is easier to think of it as above the state of experience. Wordsworth's *Ode on Intimations of Immortality* follows the same general pattern as the poems by Vaughan and Traherne·in the seventeenth century, in which the infant soul descends to a lower world. This spatial schema recurs later in Nietzsche's *Zarathustra,* in Strindberg's *Great Highway,* in Ibsen's *When We Dead Awaken,* where the mountain-top carries similar associations of an escape from the limitations of ordinary experience. But for a more conservatively pessimistic Romantic, such as Schopenhauer, it is easier to think of the structure of civilization, or the state of experience, as on top of a subhuman and submoral "world as will," an ark or *bateau ivre* carrying the cargo of human values and tossing on a stormy and threatening sea. This figure becomes the prevailing one later in the nineteenth century, both for the revolutionary optimists, with Marx at their head, who see the traditional privileges of a ruling class threatened with destruction from below, and for more sombre thinkers—Schopenhauer himself, Freud, Kierkegaard—all of whom think of the values of intelligence and imagination as above, but very precariously above, a dark, menacing, and subhuman power—Schopenhauer's world as will, Freud's id, Kierkegaard's dread. For all of these, the boat and sea image is an appropriate one, and this structure in particular shows us how the Romantic mythological schema, unlike its predecessor, enables poets and philosophers to express a man-centered revolutionary, or counter-revolutionary, attitude to society. It is Blake, as usual, who gives us the complete structure of the Romantic revolutionary myth. In his *Songs of Innocence and Experience* the child is the symbol of the state of innocence, not because he is morally good but because he is civilized: that is, he assumes that the world is protected by parents and that it is an order of nature that makes human sense. As he grows into an adult he loses this innocent vision and enters the lower world of experience. The innocent vision is then driven underground into the subconscious, as we now call it, where it becomes a subversive revolutionary force with strong sexual elements in it, which Blake calls Orc. If this force is released, it permeates the world of experience with its energy; if it is suppressed, it turns demonic.

For the quest of the soul, the attaining of man's ultimate identity, the traditional metaphors were upward ones, following the movement of the ascension of Christ, though they were there even before the Psalmist lifted up his eyes to the hills. In Romanticism the main direction of the quest of identity tends increasingly to be downward and inward, toward a hidden basis or ground of identity between man and nature. It is in a hidden region, often described in images of underground caves and streams like those of *Kubla Khan*, that the final unity between man and his nature is most often achieved. The word "dark" is thematically very important in Romanticism, especially in Germany, and it usually refers to the seeping of an identity with nature into the hidden and inner parts of the mind. Beddoes speaks of

> the depth
> *And labyrinthine home of the still soul,*
> *Where the seen thing is imaged, and the whisper*
> *Joints the expecting spirit.*

This fourth region corresponds in situation to the hell or demonic world of the previous schema, which was also usually underground, and it carries over some echoes from its predecessor, as the mysterious depths of the soul may be a place of great wickedness as well as of inner illumination, like Milton's Pandemonium with its fantastic lighting.

In the first place, the imagery of the oracular cave, so prominent in Shelley and elsewhere, is a revival of a pre-Christian mythology that goes back to the old earth-mother myths. The oracle of Apollo was taken over from an earlier female chthonic cult, but even in its reformed version it ceased to function at the coming of Christ, hence Shelley's use of such imagery indicates an anti-Christian bias. Second, the identity achieved may be with a God who is the ultimate reality of both man and nature, or it may simply be with an amoral nature. Those who manifest this inner identity are the great men, but some great men are creative and others, like Napoleon, are destructive, and there is no guarantee which form greatness will take. The ambiguity of "destroyer and preserver" is found here too. Thirdly, the only point at which one visibly enters into an identity with nature is death. Thus death is all we can usually see of what may or may not be the fullest entering into life. This paradox haunts many Romantic and post-Romantic poets. The suggestion dropped by Lucifer in Byron's *Cain*, "It may be death leads to the highest knowledge," is amplified in Beddoes and Shelley, as we shall see. In Rimbaud the poet descends not through death but through a *dérègle-ment de tous les sens* which is so sinister and disastrous that the world of identity becomes simply the old demonic world again, and the poet's sojourn in it a *saison en enfer*. Hence Rimbaud remarks that the old theologians were right after all, and that hell is downward.

The Romantic movement transforms all the generic plots of literature: there is a new and Romantic form of tragedy, of irony, of comedy: there is even—in fact there is very centrally—a new and Romantic form of romance. We shall proceed to a brief review of the Romantic developments of these four types of fictional structure, beginning with romance itself.

Conventionally, the poet is the celebrator of the hero, whose brave deeds he chronicles and whom he follows at a respectful distance. But this convention relates to a time so remote and primitive that, if it ever existed, little if any literature has survived from it. The poet, as Aristotle says, deals with the generic or universal event, not the particular historical one, and it is the hero recreated by the poet who becomes the hero of literature. As long as we have had written literature, what the poet really is directly related to in society is not the hero but a more settled order, usually presided over, in pre-Romantic times, by a prince or patron in whose court or hall the poet recites his poems or performs his dramas. In this setting the hero becomes a legendary figure from an earlier age, and predominantly a tragic figure as well, like the heroes of Ossian who went forth to battle, but always fell. This is as true of Beowulf as it is of Achilles, and it is still true of King Lear and Hamlet. In Shakespeare the balancing social figure, Queen Elizabeth or King James, remains offstage, or is symbolized in such figures of comedy as Duke Theseus in the last act of *A Midsummer Night's Dream*.

The Romantics take the next step. In their age the patron is beginning to disappear, and the poet is becoming im-

mersed in society as a whole. But though he loses his traditional specific social functions (unless he preserves them by
accident, like Goethe in Weimar), he gains a more important function, at least in his own eyes. He sees society as
held together by its creative power, incarnate in himself,
rather than by its leaders of action. Thus he himself steps
into the role of the hero, not as personally heroic but simply
as the focus of society. For him, therefore, the real event is
no longer even the universal or typical historical event,
but the psychological or mental event, the event in his own
consciousness of which the historical event is the outward
sign or allegory. This involves a rejection of history, which
becomes a "gilded cheat" in Keats, a "devil's scripture" in
Byron, and the literal Word of God (with overtones of
St. Paul's observation that the letter kills) in Blake, as the
main source of poetic fictions.

It may seem very strange to describe Romanticism as
anti-historical, when we think of how central historical
novels and narrative poems are to it. Yet when we look
more carefully at the historical fictions in Romanticism,
we see that earlier ages of history are being recreated in a
specifically Romantic form, as symbols of certain aspects of
the poet's own age. In Schiller's terms, an age thought of as
comparatively "naive" is rendered in a self-conscious or
"sentimental" way. Scott, in *Ivanhoe* and elsewhere, and,
later, William Morris both write historical fictions about
the Middle Ages. They are by no means uninformed about
the Middle Ages: Morris at least could be called a medieval specialist. But they are not interested in rendering the
Middle Ages directly. There is nothing in the language of
Middle English, for example, that corresponds even re-
motely to Morris' brocaded Teutonic diction or to Scott's
antiquated lingo. What is being rejected, one feels, is the
social reality of the earlier age; what is being preserved is

a latent or potential Utopia in it: a social ideal with some meaning for the writer's attitude to his own time. Scott is conservative, and his medieval world is an age of chivalry contrasting with his own age; Morris is radical, and his medieval world, deprived of its two pillars, church and aristocracy, is similarly an ideal age of craftsmanship confronting the nineteenth century.

Thus what is being called gilded cheat and devil's scripture is not so much history as the social process of which actual history is the record. The rejection of history in this sense is an anti-mimetic tendency, a rejecting of social reality in favor of a social ideal. The people contemporary with Romanticism that we think of as realists we also think of as outside the Romantic movement, like Crabbe in English literature. The Middle Ages itself, like all ages, had its own anti-mimetic tendencies, which it expressed in such forms as the romance, where the knight turns away from society and rides off into a forest or other "threshold symbol" of a dream world. In Romanticism this romance form revives, so significantly as to give its name to the whole movement, but in Romanticism the poet himself is the hero of the quest, and his turning away from society is to be connected with what we have been discussing, the demoting of the conception of man as primarily a social being living in cities. He turns away to seek a nature who reveals herself only to the individual.

The most comprehensive and central of all Romantic themes, then, is a romance with the poet for hero. The theme of this romance form is the attaining of an expanded consciousness, the sense of identity with God and nature which is the total human heritage, so far as the limited perspective of the human situation can grasp it. To use the traditional metaphors, the great Romantic theme is the attaining of an apocalyptic vision by a fallen but potentially regenerate mind. Such an event, taking place in an individual consciousness, may become a sign of a greater social awakening, but the latter is usually implied in it or takes place offstage. Wordsworth's *Prelude,* certainly the great Romantic epic of English literature, deals with the growth of the individual poet's mind; more social aspects of the theme were contemplated but came to very little. In Blake the great poem of individual awakening, *Milton,* is followed by *Jerusalem,* a less completely concentrated poem partly because of its attempt at a wider social vision. In *Prometheus Unbound* we are aware of the extent to which social change is symbolized by a psychological change: mankind is treated as a single gigantic individual, which Prometheus represents. Nor does Keats' *Hyperion,* as we have it, get beyond the moment of Apollo's self-awareness, though the Moneta passages in the revised version indicate Keats' sense of the importance of the social side of his subject.

It seems as though Romanticism finds it difficult to absorb the social perspective, and we notice that the poems that deal with the attaining of integrated consciousness often tend to by-pass the more realistic tragic, ironic, and comic themes. The "romantic" has in popular speech a reputation for taking a facile or rose-colored view of things, and even great works of Romanticism sometimes show us a mental quest achieved without having passed through any real difficulties or dangers on the way. A reader completely unsympathetic to, for example, the conception of the quest of the soul set out in Bunyan's *Pilgrim's Progress* could still appreciate the honesty and realism of the Slough of Despond, the Valley of the Shadow of Death, or the dungeons of Giant Despair. In contrast, Wordsworth's *Excursion* employs the normally tragic or ironic figure of the Wanderer; but Wordsworth is so nervous about the tragic and ironic aspects of experience explored, for example, by Byron, so anxious to "correct despondency" and avoid the seductions of a Voltairean spirit of mockery, that *The Excursion* impresses us more as a barrier against the great adventure of the soul than an account of it. *The Prelude* is, of course, infinitely more successful, complete and flexible, but the more tragic Vaudracour and Julia episode is cut out of the 1850 version even of that poem. Later, Matthew Arnold omitted *Empedocles on Etna* from his 1853 collection, on the grounds, really, that it added an ironic dimension to his poetry which gave him great uneasiness.

Carlyle, in *Sartor Resartus,* gives us a Romantic quest of the soul which passes through a tragic and Wertherean "Everlasting No," an ironic and Byronic "Centre of Indifference," and finally reaches an "Everlasting Yea." The last is, in the first place, the identifying of the individual, symbolized, in the "sartor resartus" imagery, by George Fox's self-made suit of leather. This stage corresponds in Wordsworth to the vision of the leech-gatherer in *Resolution and Independence,* whose self-sufficiency corrects the melancholy of the poet. There follows, in Carlyle, the integrating of the identified individual, through his productive capacities, with society. Carlyle deserves every credit for attempting to unite the social with the individual perspective, but unfortunately he reverts to the older conception of the hero as the center of society, to whom the rest of us, including the poet, have first of all to relate.

There are two types of such leaders: leaders *de jure,* royal or aristocratic figures like the Duke Theseus of Shakespeare, who symbolize the unity of their society, and leaders *de facto,* represented by the "captains of industry" in Carlyle's day and by earlier *tyrannos* figures like Napoleon, Cromwell, and Frederick the Great. This perspective was the natural one for Shakespeare's historical plays, but for a Romantic poet, who sees society in relation to the creative rather than the kinetic function, it is an anachronism. And because Carlyle endorses, rather than simply observing, the view he adopts, one has a nagging feeling that his hero-worship is not only anachronistic but literally mistaken: the authentic form of what was later to be called the *trahison des clercs*. When we look more closely at his view of the hero we see one reason why it is mistaken: in literature the hero is normally and naturally a tragic figure, and Carlyle's conception of the hero is associated with a vulgar fear of tragedy. All his heroes must be successful: if a great spirit appears in history, things ought not to go wrong, and, by the same view, any man who makes a considerable mark in history must be a hero.

We should expect to find tragic, ironic, and comic themes, because of their more social and realistic setting, less completely developed in Romanticism, but there are of course great Romantic contributions in all three areas, especially in tragedy. From what we have said about Romantic mythology, we should expect the dominant form of Romantic tragedy to be the tragedy of self-awareness, the sense of losing the spontaneity of one's relationship to nature and becoming an isolated and subjective consciousness. The story of Faust, disillusioned with everything that the conscious mind can give him, feeling that he wants nothing except a return to a youthful state of spontaneity and yet finding his conscious awareness betraying him once more, is a central Romantic tragedy. Pre-Romantic tragedy was concerned mainly with the hero as social leader: even the most psychological studies of a sick society in Jacobean dramatists still keep their central figures inseparable from their communities and their social functions. The theme of the disintegration of society is essential even to *Hamlet,* which makes the closest approach to the Romantic preoccupation with the excess of conscious awareness over the power of action. Romantic tragedies of course often retain the general form and structure of pre-Romantic tragedy, if only out of respect for its prestige, but their central figures are more likely to reflect the vogue of the "Byronic" hero already glanced at, the hero who is placed outside the structure of civilization and therefore represents the force of physical nature, amoral or ruthless, yet with a sense of power, and often of leadership, that society has impoverished itself by rejecting.

Another modulation of this type is the exile or wanderer, who is usually isolated by an introverted quality of mind. Byron's Childe Harold, the Ancient Mariner, and Shelley's Alastor and Wandering Jew figures show us, in very different contexts, aspects of the tragic situation, from a Romantic point of view, of being detached from society and its conventional values. None of these characters are thinkers: they are brooders or visionaries, but the convention often assumes that they are thinkers, centers of a mental activity too intense for social intercourse. Thus Childe Harold:

> *Yet must I think less wildly:—I have thought*
> *Too long and darkly, till my brain became,*
> *In its own eddy boiling and o'erwrought,*
> *A whirling gulf of phantasy and flame.*

Notice how natural it is for a Romantic poet to use the word "darkly" in connection with thought. The archetype of all such brooding outcasts is Rousseau, and Rousseau's *Confessions* illustrates two recurring features of the Romantic tragic formula. The formula often expresses itself in a confessional genre, where the main figure is apt to be a perfunctory mask for the author himself, and it often uses the image of the lost mother as a symbol for the fall into excessive awareness. The role of various maternal figures in Rousseau, notably Madame de Warens, has much more than a simply biographical significance. Perhaps the overtones of "Childe" in Childe Harold also have echoes beyond the allusion to medieval romance: certainly Byron himself, and his publisher, were well aware of the appeal of such heroes to women readers.

Other confessional forms, such as De Quincey's *Confessions of an English Opium-Eater,* gain considerably in significance if one relates them to their proper context. We said that the central theme of Romanticism is that of the attaining of an expanded consciousness, and this phrase, to a reader in the nineteen-sixties, suggests current talk about the virtues of LSD and marijuana. But even from the point of view of Romanticism with its isolated visionaries, there is still a distinction between the genuine or creative consciousness and the introverted or subjective one. De Quincey's account of his miserable exile from the maternal figure of Lady Carbery, of his sterile union in bitter cold with Ann, and of the way in which his vision broke up, under the influence of opium, into a shower of tantalizing and elusive glimpses, is, seen in relation to Romanticism as a whole, one of the profoundest and most moving of Romantic autobiographical tragedies.

Traditionally, the tragedy, or at least the Renaissance European tragedy, has been polarized by two themes: social heroism and sexual passion. The tragic hero of Romanticism is usually a tragic lover, and here again it is an excess of consciousness, which isolates the lover instead of uniting him to his beloved, that causes the tragedy. What begins as love ends in frustration, torment, or suicide. The convention is the old convention of Courtly Love, where the mistress may kill her lover with her "cruelty," but the treatment of the convention emphasizes rather the lover's growing morbid awareness of what would now be called the metaphysical absurd. This theme gives us the Werther syndrome in Romantic literature, of which Ugo Foscolo's *Ultime lettere di Jacopo Ortis,* and, with a less rigorous conclusion, Constant's *Adolphe* and Hazlitt's *Liber Amoris* are other examples. Genuinely tragic themes, as distinct from ironic ones, are relatively rare in Romantic literature, partly because they come so close to placing the poet himself in a heroic but defeated role. Perhaps we have to wait for Proust before we find the full tragic counterpart to the great Romantic epics: Proust's account of a growing consciousness which, like Wordsworth's, has intermittent flashes of paradisal vision, but finally realizes that there are no paradises except lost ones, that this realization confers on the narrator the tragic dimension of defeated heroism, the ability to see mankind as giants immersed in time, and that maturity means among other things the irreparable and final loss of the mother.

Romantic irony revolves around de Sade and the so-called "Romantic agony," the sense of the interpenetration of pleasure and pain, beauty and evil, intensity and destructiveness. There are two chief recurring characters. One is an exile or outcast figure similar to the one that we find in tragic stories, except that he is without the support that nature gives to the more genuinely tragic hero's contest with society. The ironic outcast is rather a *desdichado* figure, a sad Quixote whose aristocratic pretensions are an illusion. His female counterpart is an elusive or sinister *femme fatale,* the Romantic embodiment of the cruel mistress of Courtly Love.

It is unfortunate that Praz's influential book concentrates so much on the purely psychological elements of sadism, for sadism is far more important as a sardonic parody of the Rousseauist view of society. According to de Sade, nature teaches us that the greatest good of life is pleasure, and there is no keener pleasure than the inflicting (or, for masochists, who complete the theory, the suffering) of pain. A society of sadistic masters and masochistic slaves would therefore be a "natural" society. There is no evidence that Rousseau's natural society ever did, could, or will exist: the evidence that it is natural for man to form societies that condemn the majority to misery and humiliation and give a small group the privilege of enjoying their torments is afforded by the whole of human history. The sense that ecstasy and pain are really the same thing is connected with the fact, just mentioned, that for Romantic mythology the greatest experiences of life originate in a world which is also the world of death and destruction.

For the great ironic developments that come out of Romanticism we have to turn to a later poetic tradition that begins with Baudelaire and a fictional one that begins with Flaubert. In English there is of course Byron's *Don Juan,* which belongs to the more militantly ironic form of satire, Byron having an affinity with the more realistic age of Pope that makes him unique among English Romantics. Shelley's *Cenci*, depicting Beatrice's revolt against the sadistic onslaughts of her father, is revolutionary so far as it creates a dramatic sympathy for Beatrice, and ironic so far as it portrays her as involved in the evil she fights against. An almost equally remarkable example of Romantic irony is Mary Shelley's *Frankenstein*. This story is not, as it is often said to be, a precursor of science fiction: it is a precursor rather of the existential thriller, of such a book as Camus' *L'Etranger*. The whole point about the monster is that he is not a machine, but an ordinary human being isolated from mankind by extreme ugliness, Blake's "different face." The number of allusions to *Paradise Lost* in

the narrative indicate that the story is a retelling of the
account of the origin of evil, in a world where the only
creators that we can locate are human ones. Frankenstein
hunts down his monster in the same way that moral good
attempts to destroy the moral evil it has itself created:
Frankenstein is quite as much a death-principle as his
quarry, and is surrounded by the vengeful spirits of the
monster's victims.

The traditional structure of comedy is one which leads
up to the birth of a new society, usually crystallizing
around the marriage of the hero and the heroine, in the
conventional "happy ending" of the final scene. Certain in-
dividuals whose behavior is threatening or eccentric, misers,
bragging soldiers, tyrannical parents, and the like, try to
obstruct this ending and are thwarted or converted. Comedy restructures society by expanding it and making it
more flexible; it exhibits the individual as eccentric and
makes society triumph over him. It thus tends to be a realistic form with a strongly social emphasis which is not particularly congenial to Romanticism. The novels of Jane
Austen are pure comedies, and for that reason not quite
what we think of as typically Romantic. There is, however, one form of comedy which Romanticism has more in
common with, and that, as we should expect, is the "romantic" comedy of Shakespeare. Shakespeare often presents
his action in the form of a collision of two societies, one the
ordinary society of experience, generally a court, the other
a mysterious world often associated with magic and fairies,
with strongly erotic and Dionysian overtones. In the Romantic comedies this world, represented, for example, by
the forest of Arden in *As You Like It,* the wood of Oberon
in *A Midsummer Night's Dream,* Portia's house in *The
Merchant of Venice,* establishes an ascendancy over the
other world and forces a comic conclusion on it. Shake-

spearean comedy has clearly been a strong influence on *Prometheus Unbound* and *Endymion* at least. But even in Shakespeare the emphasis is social, and Romantic comedy takes rather the individual form, the attaining of an expanded consciousness, already spoken of. Thus, in Romanticism, comedy and the successful completing of the romance quest tend to be much the same form.

To sum up: any given literature is rooted in a specific culture and is contained by the mythological structure of that culture. Pre-Romantic literature in Western Europe was contained by a structure that, for the critical purpose of interpreting the imagery of poetry, is best understood as a structure on four spatial levels, though of course if it were interpreted differently, by a philosopher or a theologian, there would not literally be any levels or places. These four levels are heaven, the unfallen world which is man's original and proper home, the ordinary world of experience, and the demonic world of eternal death. In this schema there are two principles involved, one cyclical and the other dialectical. The two levels of nature in the middle are related cyclically: imagery of fertility, youth and perpetual spring, and gardens of flourishing trees and flowing water describe the world man fell from at the beginning of the cycle of history, and to which he should return at the end of it. Heaven and hell, on the other hand, are worlds of eternal separation, one being a community of identity and the other a pseudo-community of alienation. These two worlds are normally, in poetic imagery, "up" and "down," associated respectively with the starry skies and the underground world of the dead.

Romanticism brought in a new mythological construction. We can still think of it as a four-tiered structure, but it is much less concretely related to the physical world as we ordinarily perceive it. What corresponds to heaven and hell is still there, the worlds of identity and of alienation, but the imagery associated with them, being based on the opposition of "within" and "without" rather than of "up" and "down," is almost reversed. The identity "within," being not purely subjective but a communion, whether with nature or God, is often expressed in imagery of depth or descent. (In contemporary theology there appears to be a determined effort to get rid of "up there" metaphors in relation to God, but somehow it sounds right to say that God is the "ground" of being.) On the other hand, the sense of alienation is reinforced, if anything, by the imagery of what, since Pascal, has increasingly been felt to be the terrifying waste spaces of the heavens.

The two inner worlds of nature, human nature and physical nature, are also still there, but their relation to each other is also usually reversed. In pre-Romantic imagery the world of social and civilized life, however evil or corrupt, and however thoroughly denounced, was still the gateway to identity: man for pre-Romantic poets was still primarily a social and civilized being and could not progress except through his social heritage. In a great deal of Romantic imagery human society is thought of as leading to alienation rather than identity, and this sense increases steadily throughout the nineteenth century as literature becomes more ironic in both tone and structure. In Romanticism there is an emphasis on the false identity of the conforming group—even for the most conservative Romantics the real social values are in a tradition which has probably been lost anyway—and, by contrast, on a kind of creative and healing alienation to be gained from a solitary contact with the order of nature outside society. For many writers today this sense of creative alienation has disappeared, and only the ironic view of society remains. But the Romantic appeal to nature is a mighty force yet, even in an age when "nature" has become practically reduced to the human sexual instinct.

The difficulty we mentioned in Romanticism of incorporating a social theme with the theme of individual enlightenment is still with us. Romanticism has brought into modern consciousness the feeling that society can develop or progress only by individualizing itself, by being sufficiently tolerant and flexible to allow an individual to find his own identity within it, even though in doing so he comes to repudiate most of the conventional values of that society. The bourgeois democracies of America and Western Europe, Marxist countries, and fascist and nationalist movements, all of which have political principles derived from different aspects of Romantic mythology translated into programs of social action, have tried to overcome this situation in different ways, sometimes with the help of some of the poets, as our comments on Carlyle show. But the residual anarchism at the heart of the Romantic movement is still with us, and will be until society stops trying to suppress it.

+ + +

What follows are brief studies of the structure and imagery of three major works of English Romantic literature. The sequence is not chronological, but is a series of phases of myth, in which each work in the sequence takes in a wider scope than its predecessor. All three are works of second-generation Romanticism, and all three take a liberal, sometimes a revolutionary attitude to religion and politics, in which the break with the older symbolic language is easier to see. Beddoes revolves around the heart of Romantic imagery, at the point of identity with nature of which death is the only visible form. Shelley deals with the theme of Romantic comedy as outlined above, the regenerating of the alienated community through a renewed understanding of nature as the complement of humanity. The theme of Keats' *Endymion* is the bringing to birth of the imagination as the focus of society. The whole sequence should give some idea of the range and scope of the mythical structure within which the literature of our own day is still operating, and which with the Romantic movement completed its first major phase.

Yorick:
The Romantic Macabre

The masterpiece of Thomas Lovell Beddoes, *Death's Jest-Book,* never seems really to have been integrated into the study of Romanticism. The reasons are partly a matter of biographical accident. The poet published *The Bride's Tragedy* in 1822: Shelley and Keats were dead, Byron was soon to follow them, and Beddoes became with this work their only immediate successor on anything like their level of achievement. Contrary to the usual practice of Romantic criticism when faced with genius, *The Bride's Tragedy* was generously praised, and Beddoes was well launched as a poet. He then began several other projects, including *Death's Jest-Book,* the first version of which was apparently complete by 1829. But instead of publishing it then, and making it the bridge between Keats and the early Tennyson, he kept working at it and revising it until his suicide in 1849. As he had been living in Germany and studying medicine, he had become a somewhat peripheral figure in English literature by the time of his death. Hence *Death's Jest-Book* crept into English poetry almost unnoticed, an easy victim for the kind of generalizer who calls it "morbid." To put such an epithet against this gorgeous plum-pudding of a poem, filled to bursting with heady lines and breath-taking images, is a sufficient comment on the accuracy of critical clichés.

From the beginning Beddoes was possessed, not so much by death, as by the idea of the identity of death and love, Thanatos and Eros. Both states are themselves identifications of an isolated and conscious being with something else not itself. The imagery of such songs as "Dirge and Hymeneal" or "The Two Archers" tells us that the darts of love and death are aimed at the same target, that all lovers are demon-lovers, all brides incarnations of Mother Earth. Frustration in love (as the character Athulf, in *Death's Jest-Book,* shows us in particular) is very apt to turn into a death-wish. Thus the highest and most intense aspects of life, which love represents, are not the opposite of death, but part of the drive toward death which is the momentum of life itself. The complete identity with nature, which is the fulfillment of life, is achieved visibly only by death; hence death is the most accurate symbol of the ultimate meaning of life.

The question whether life drives *to* death or *through* it remains, for most of us, an unanswerable question. Beddoes answers, not that there is a "life after" death, but that life and death are different aspects of the same world, related as day is to night, summer to winter. Man, says Beddoes, is the seed of a ghost, and just as Samuel Butler remarks that a chicken is an egg's way of producing another egg, so Beddoes presents us with a world in which a human life is a ghost's way of producing another ghost. The matter is not as straightforward as this, even in Beddoes, but one principle is clear enough to go on with. In our account of the Romantic myth we spoke of two orders of nature, one the world of ordinary social human experience, the other a world connected with uncultivated nature, the physical environment outside society. This latter world is the world of the "sublime," and it is Wordsworth's benevolent teacher, but we noted that in later Romanticism it is often more pessimistically regarded. It becomes, for example, Schopenhauer's world as will. Beddoes makes a startling and yet oddly suggestive identification. For him the world of experience is the world of life, which has its focus and climax in love, and the world outside it becomes, quite simply, the world of death. The demon-lover theme is thus, in his work, the symbol of a life-death identity which he calls eternity. This identity can manifest itself only in the form of an antithesis, the antithesis we know as life *and* death. Its main symbol in Beddoes, as so often elsewhere in Romanticism, is that of the struggle of brothers, of which one represents ordinary life driving toward death, the other death seeping back into life.

The Bride's Tragedy is based on the theme of the demon-lover. The villain-hero, significantly named Hesperus, loves Floribel, who is called a nymph of the wood and is associated with Diana. Their secret meeting at sunset in the forest opens the play, and it soon becomes clear that, for Hesperus, Floribel is going to be not a Diana but a Proserpine. A story is told about a bee and a red rose with the conventional dying-god conclusion:

> *the guilty blossom*
> *His heart's blood stained.*

Certain thematic images are established: there is the imagery of flowers and wind, which are associated with love
and death respectively, and of a false paradise where everything is dark, hidden, and possessed in secret, and where
grapes and poison fruit are near together. The ominous
images set a tone which leads up to the murder of Floribel.
Hesperus is provided by Beddoes with three sets of motiva-
tions for his act: one, his father is imprisoned by a Duke
who wants Floribel for himself and is trying to force Hesperus into marrying his sister Olivia; two, Hesperus sees
Floribel kissing a page boy and is seized with irrational
jealousy in the regular Beaumont and Fletcher convention; and three, most interesting of all, he has a Freudian
trauma: in infancy he lay on his nurse's breast when she
was killed by a lightning bolt, which inspires him with
a cyclical madness. This last, in particular, has possessed
him with the sense of the identity of birth, love, and death.
After he kills Floribel he turns to Olivia, but the same secret and possessive imagery recurs ("We'll build a wall between us and the world"), and he speaks also to her of
death as the real consummation of love as well as of life:

> *For when our souls are born then will we wed;*
> *Our dust shall mix and grow into one stalk.*

There is also a suggestion of a cycle of death moving opposite to the cycle of life, of ghosts begetting ghosts. To
nerve himself for his murder Hesperus stands on the grave
of another murderer, and feels the latter's spirit passing
into himself. We understand that the real murderous impulse is within him: as the Duke shrewdly remarks:

> *'Tis but one devil ever tempts a man,*
> *And his name's* Self.

And yet one feels that there is something sacrificial about all the deaths in the play, the direction of the sacrifice being not, as with ritual sacrifice, to safeguard the living, but to strengthen the community of death. Hints are thrown out about forms of life beyond life, and Olivia's attendant tries, as she says, to

> *persuade myself this intercourse*
> *Of disembodied minds is no conjecture,*
> *No fiction of romance.*

And although Hesperus goes through agonies of remorse and other appropriate emotions, he seems oddly to have extended his experience by his crime in a way that makes it something more than merely a crime.

Of various dramatic fragments that Beddoes began shortly after *The Bride's Tragedy,* the most remarkable, and the most nearly completed, is *The Second Brother,* over four acts of which survive. There are really three brothers in this play: a Duke of Ferrara, who dies without appearing in the action; Marcello, the next oldest, an exile presumed dead; and Orazio, the heir apparent by default. The action opens with the return of Marcello and his encounter with Orazio. The encounter is in the tonality of death confronting life, the skeleton or death's head at the scene of festivity. Orazio, handsome, popular, extravagant, with all eyes on him, is brought up short in his public triumph by his beggared brother. In this moment of contact they symbolize the opposition of living and dead worlds, as Marcello says:

We are like two mountain peaks
Of two close planets, catching in the air:
You, King Olympus, a great pile of summer,
Wearing a crown of gods; I, the vast top
Of the ghosts' deadly world, naked and dark.

Several other contrasts are involved, including one rather like that of Mark Antony and Octavius. Orazio is a Dionysus, a lord of love and wine, spilling over with life and energy; Marcello is a votary of Apollo, who prays to a god he thinks of as remote and withdrawn:

Great solitary god of that one sun,
I charge thee by the likeness of our state.

As an "Apollonian" he stands for order, form, everything that is fixed in a place. He is also the Jupiter of the earth and heaven, as Orazio is the Neptune of the liquid world. In this last set of archetypes the dying Duke would correspond to the Pluto gone to the shades below. As the rivalry develops, Orazio's extravagance leads him to bankruptcy and Marcello succeeds to the dukedom, recognized as the rightful heir. Another demon-lover theme then develops, centered on the heroine Valeria, who is apparently about to be murdered when the main fragment ends.

These two themes, the demon-lover whose love is death and the two brothers who symbolize the two orders of nature, the living and dead worlds, are combined in *Death's Jest-Book*. The central idea of this play is that of death as fool, an invisible jester who appears only in the form of a grinning skull, like Shakespeare's Yorick. This idea is announced in a verse letter to a friend written in 1826, where Beddoes says that his play will not only rob death of all his traditional terrors, but will actually make "a mock, a fool, a slave of him," and that the action will show him as a comic butt or "unmask'd braggart." The doctrine that death is unreal, that it is properly to be regarded as comfort, and that it is a major obstacle to human development to "believe in" death, appears already in *The Bride's Tragedy* in a speech by Olivia—in Beddoes it is usually the heroine who attains these intuitions. But Beddoes seems to have felt, at least at this time, that his medical studies gave scientific support to his beliefs: "I owe this wisdom to Anatomy," he says. To regard death as something so impotent that it can actually be treated like a *miles gloriosus* indicates an optimism, if that is the word, so intolerable that one doubts if any serious poet, least of all Beddoes, could give sustained expression to it. Shakespeare does use the term fool in the passive sense of comic butt, meaning someone who cannot control events, in such phrases as "time's fool" or "the natural fool of fortune." But death is not Beddoes' fool in this sense: on the contrary, he is the undisputed victor of the play's action. The wisdom of anatomy may have let Beddoes down, but in any case his poetic instinct would have led him to a much more ambiguous treatment of the death-fool theme than he suggests here.

The plot of *Death's Jest-Book*, which was not essentially altered by revision, revolves around two brothers, Wolfram and Isbrand, disguised as a knight and a court-fool respectively, in the service of Melveric, Duke of Münsterberg. Isbrand has a melancholy and sardonic temperament like the "malcontent" type popularized by Marston: more generally, he is the kind of highly articulate tragic hero who can act as chorus to his own action, of the family of Hamlet, Bosola, and Vendice. Isbrand is dedicated to revenge on the Duke, who has killed their father: Wolfram, a saintly and chivalric spirit, has renounced revenge and in a complicated action, which takes place in Egypt, saves the

Duke's life after the Duke has tried to poison him, out of rivalry over the heroine Sibylla. Exasperated by Wolfram's invulnerable virtue and his sense of inferiority to it, the Duke finally succeeds in murdering him and returns to Münsterberg with Sibylla, followed by Isbrand. Once home, the Duke's love slips back to the memory of his dead wife, in a way typical of Beddoes' dramatic actions. Similarly, Hesperus can only love what he is about to try to destroy, and Orazio does not really love the heroine Valeria until after he has neglected her to the verge of killing her with a broken heart.

The late Duchess' body, in a grisly scene, is exchanged for that of Wolfram by Isbrand. The Duke attempts to call up the ghost of his wife by necromancy; he thus, because of the exchange, calls up Wolfram instead, who cannot be dismissed because he has been definitely summoned. Wolfram's ghost, like the Sweet William of the ballads, renews his earthly love for the now neglected Sibylla, who dies to join him. Isbrand organizes a conspiracy against the Duke and is temporarily successful, but once vested with authority he becomes tyrannical. The main action for the latter half of the play shifts to the Duke's two sons, the dutiful and heroic Adalmar and the self-indulgent Athulf. Isbrand has planned their deaths as part of his revenge, but their love for the same woman, Amala, which repeats the main theme in counterpoint, leads to the same climax, with Athulf murdering his brother. In the amazing final scene, where a *danse macabre* painted on the walls of a crypt comes to life, Athulf stabs himself, Isbrand is killed by a blind devotee of liberty named Mario, and Wolfram, who replaces Isbrand as fool in the last scene, pulls the Duke down into his grave, "still alive, into the world of the dead," "dead" being appropriately the last word in the play. This account gives little indication of the skill with which Beddoes manages to make all these deaths individually plausible and cumulatively convincing to the emotions.

It has been noticed that every great Romantic poet in English literature leaves some major and central work unfinished, or revises and reworks it incessantly. The reasons naturally vary, but some features recur. Byron's *Childe Harold* and *Don Juan* are unfinished because they are, in very different moods, parodies of the Romantic completed quest. That is, they are endless poems in their very inception, and could only be abandoned when the author tired of the persona. Keats' *Hyperion,* Blake's *Four Zoas,* and Wordsworth's *Prelude* were revised and reworked partly because they were, in a sense, definitive poems, expressing the heart of what their creators had to say. Both these reasons apply to *Death's Jest-Book,* and with Beddoes something also has to be allowed for personal temperament. He tells us little about himself in his letters, but a tone of self-deprecation recurs which suggests some doubts about his ability ever to finish his work to his own satisfaction. There is nothing neurotic in his writing, but an increasingly self-destructive streak in him, which destroyed first a large body of his work and then his life, links him more closely than any other English Romantic to some of the tormented and self-mutilated geniuses of German Romanticism, such as Kleist and Hölderlin. A more technical reason for the long delay in giving *Death's Jest-Book* to the world, however, was Beddoes' desire to make it a real stage play, to be acted in a theater. True, there was an audience for verse tragedies in his time—Keats even had a notion that *Otho the Great* would make money—but it is hard to see how *Death's Jest-Book* could have succeeded on the stage. Yet, before we assign Beddoes to that unhappy, obsessed, and somewhat masochistic band of modern poets who have tried to "revive poetic drama," we should glance at the courage and common sense with which he defines his attitude:

> I am convinced the man who is to awaken the drama must be a bold trampling fellow . . . With the greatest reverence for all the antiquities of the drama, I still think we had better beget than revive—attempt to give the literature of this age an idiosyncrasy and spirit of its own, and only raise a ghost to gaze on, not to live with.

Beddoes had learned from the dramatists of Shakespeare's age how an intense concentration on scenes of horror and violence impregnates the tragic with a comic mood that T. S. Eliot calls "farce," and recognizes in *The Jew of Malta*. Similarly, although *Death's Jest-Book* is subtitled "The Fool's Tragedy," its pervading tone is not so much tragic as a combination of the tragic and the comic which we may call the grotesque. What Beddoes was trying for was a tragic action based on the mood of the porter scene in *Macbeth,* or, again, the grave-digging scene in *Hamlet* in which Yorick, or at least his skull, appears. Perhaps it is really the discovery of the tragicomic grotesque that Beddoes is announcing in the verse letter referred to above, a discovery as crucial for him as that of the comic rhyme was for Byron.

The root of the conception of the grotesque is the sense of the simultaneous presence of life and death. Ghosts, for example, are at once alive and dead, and so inspire the kind of hysteria that is expressed equally by horror and by laughter. The grotesque is also the expression in literature of the nauseated vision, man's contemplating of himself as a mortal body who returns to nature as "dung and death," in the phrase of *East Coker*. Death, so far as it is a physical process, is always firmly attached by Beddoes to complete dissolution and a return to the nitrogen cycle: "Turning to daisies gently in the grave." The most concentrated symbol of this aspect of the grotesque is perhaps the cannibal feast, the subject of two strategically placed lyrics in the play, one sung by Isbrand and the other by Wolfram, both in their character as fools. Isbrand's song "Harpagus, hast thou salt enough?" deals with the theme, used by Seneca in *Thyestes* and imported into Shakespeare's *Titus Andronicus,* of serving up an enemy's children to him as food, traditionally the most shocking of all tragic themes, and therefore close not only to tragedy but to "farce," in Eliot's sense. The other song uses the slightly less nauseating theme of ravens eating dead bodies: the ravens, however, are called Adam and Eve. Other similar images evoke a vision o nature as a vast cannibal banquet of the same kind, a Hieronymus Bosch landscape in which men turn into animals and animals into men. As Isbrand says:

> Some one of those malicious Gods who envy Prometheus his puppet show have taught all confounded sorts of malcontent beasts, saucy birds and ambitious shellfish, and hopping creatures of land and water, the knack of looking human to the life. How? is the mystery of the cookery-book.

The conception of the grotesque, and more particularly the conception of death as fool, takes us back to the practice of medieval and Renaissance courts of collecting fools, dwarfs, cripples, and the like to serve the purpose of a *memento mori.* Man is the only animal that knows he is going to die: this consciousness is now regarded as the source of anxiety (*Angst*), and hence, usually, as something feared and to be avoided, even (if not especially) in thought. Elaborate defense mechanisms against the awareness of death are among the commonest reactions to the human situation: one of the most elaborate is the associating of death with dignity or purity, as in the description of the death of Little Nell. The insistence on the grotesque was not much liked in Beddoes' day: one thinks of Bagehot's somewhat prissy comments on the grotesque in Browning, and of the resentment aroused by the appearance of the same theme in Beddoes' great contemporary Edgar Allan Poe. He who could write *King Pest,* said the horrified Stevenson, had ceased to be a human being.

But Beddoes is a portent of a change in sensibility, also marked by the absorption of Poe into Baudelaire, which regards the grotesque as exuberant rather than "morbid." All genuine humor in one sense is gallows humor, because humor begins in the accepting of the limits of the human condition. The desire for knowledge may begin as a revolt against the consciousness of death, but being directed toward the conquest of the unknown and mysterious, and the ultimate unknown mystery being death, the goal of the impulse to know becomes the same as its source. In a world where the process of living is the same thing as the process of dying, knowledge interpenetrates with the absurd; hence wisdom is identical with folly. "He who hath no leaven of the original father Donkey in any corner of him," says a "zany" named Homunculus Mandrake, who supplies some ghoulish comic relief in the play, "may be an angel, black, white or piebald: he has lost title to humanity." We shall see later how important this antagonism to "angelism" is in the argument of the play.

What is distinctive and most original about Beddoes' version of the grotesque is his realization that normal waking consciousness is a deliberately chosen point of view, and that other points of view are conceivable. If life interpenetrates with death, then sanity interpenetrates with insanity, and waking with dreaming. To explore such a theme a poet needs what Beddoes, alone of the great English Romantics, had: the distinctively modern quality of fantasy. To come back to *Death's Jest-Book* as a stage play, Beddoes saw clearly that tragedy could not be permanently "revived" except in a grotesque, and consequently anti-heroic, context. To attempt a play in which death has the role of jester makes Beddoes a precursor of the theater of the absurd.

It was hardly possible for Beddoes to create such a theater in his time, but it is easiest to understand certain features of *Death's Jest-Book* in the light of later theatrical developments. The play begins with an epigraph from Aristophanes' *Frogs,* and *The Frogs* is perhaps closest of any earlier play to Beddoes in its portrayal of a world of the dead related to the world of life in a way that makes us wonder which is really which. Beddoes' characters live in a kind of subterranean world like that of Eliot's *Waste Land,* where the life of ordinary consciousness is, like the life of the isolated Ancient Mariner, a life in death, the cemetery of reality. The ship which carries the chief characters from Egypt to Germany is called the Baris, the name of Charon's ferry-boat in the underworld, and the fact that Isbrand and the Duke are both in disguise helps to emphasize the feeling that the actors are "hollow men," or shadows. Wolfram the ghost is no more but no less solid than the other characters; Ziba, the necromancer who is the Duke's servant, is said to have been found in the underworld, and Mandrake expresses the complementary view about living people: "there is many a fellow with broad shoulders and a goodly paunch who looks and behaves as if he were alive, although in soul and spirit he be three times more dead than salt fish in Lent."

We are constantly in a twilight world between life and death, like the world of Beckett, or a world between physical objects and mysterious forces of which the objects are symbols, like the world of Ionesco, or a world like the "Bardo" world between death and rebirth which Yeats imported from the Orient. One of the most haunting songs in the play is actually about reincarnation, in its grotesque form of rebirth into animals, and the three characters we meet in the first scene, Mandrake the zany, whose name of Homunculus suggests something deformed or dwarfish, the saintly Wolfram, and the court-fool Isbrand, remind us of the approaching chaos of the end of Yeats' lunar cycle of which "hunchback and saint and fool are the final crescents." Yeatsian too is the sense of a world moving from life to death interpenetrating with another world moving in the reverse direction through dreams, in a continuous weaving shuttle or "double gyre."

The characters in Elizabethan and Jacobean tragedy, however melancholy and withdrawn in temperament they may be, are, we said earlier, always essentially related to a society. But the characters in Beddoes are essentially lost in themselves, like the characters in Chekhov or Strindberg. One occasionally feels, perhaps, that, as often in Dickens, the complicated plot is not the natural narrative sequence of the action, but a force externally applied to keep the action moving and interrelated. The characters are not acting out what they are but are being made to do things, like a social gathering organized into games and charades instead of being left to conversation. We shall return to this point, but we have to recognize that this movement of spasmodic and galvanized action, of characters driven into complications of incident by their passions as helplessly as inanimate objects, is a part of Beddoes' conception of the play, and of human action in general.

It is connected too with a philosophical cast of mind which reminds us of Seneca, especially in the way that Bed-

does associates heroism more with consciousness than with
action. It is the mind that triumphs or gets defeated rather
than the will, even when the character is pre-eminently a
man of action, as the Duke is. We are still in the Romantic
area where the poetic imagination is the real center and
the hero is projected from it. Beddoes is Senecan too in
the way that a uniform rhetorical texture seems to oblit-
erate most of the differences in the speaking idioms of the
characters. Part of this is a melodramatic tendency which
Beddoes shares with most of the tragic drama of his time,
and which shows itself in the creation not of individual but
of romantic and stylized characters: stock heroes and vil-
lains and heroines and comic servants. Such characters are
archetypes in a Jungian sense, with the glow of projection around them: Sibylla, for instance, the heroine, is a
Jungian anima-figure, as Ziba, the Duke's slave, is a Jungian "shadow."

In a sense the Romantic rejection of the social process
as the center of human reality, already mentioned, would,
carried to its logical limits, make any original drama except
some form of the drama of the absurd ultimately impos-
sible. The curious treatment of historical period in *Death's
Jest-Book* is interesting and typical. The action of the play
is said to take place in the thirteenth century, although the
use of the *danse macabre* brings it closer to the fifteenth: it
occasionally sounds rather like an *Everyman* rewritten by
Dunbar. For it was when the medieval world began to
break up that the *danse macabre* became popular, partly
as a form of social protest. Death the leveler, who came
equally to emperor and clown, was the only visible demo-
crat, the only effective reminder of human equality. Beddoes' political sympathies, which were liberal by British
standards and practically revolutionary by Continental
ones, are consistent with his treatment of death. But the

real setting is simply Romantic Gothic, and its atmosphere is not that of a definite period of the past, but of a historical essence suspended in time, like the curious Roman-Renaissance background of Shakespeare's *Cymbeline*. There are some deliberate anachronisms, references to Columbus and to English critics, and Mario, the blind man who kills Isbrand, has "seen" the assassination of Julius Caesar, perhaps not wholly in imagination. People move about with the dignity, passion, and rhetoric of a generalized traditional past: the absence of any definite historical community is one of the things that create the sense of something alive and dead at the same time. The feeling is similar to the later romances of William Morris and the Celtic twilight period of Yeats, except that there is much less sense of subjectivity: Beddoes differs from them somewhat as Strindberg differs from Maeterlinck.

The tendency to fragmentation in Beddoes' work generally is another significant feature. We may sometimes wonder whether Beddoes, like Goethe, was less of a serious dramatist than a great lyrical poet who was primarily interested, not in the overall dramatic structure, but in decentralized emotional foci, especially those of the interspersed songs. The lyrical element in the play actually increased as Beddoes went on revising it: some of the finest of the songs are later additions. Further, death is the fool, and one of the functions of the fool is to act as a "touchstone," whose jokes indicate something central in the characters of others. Death as fool is a touchstone in this way: everyone dies, as he has lived, in a way distinctive of himself. The speech uttered at the point of death in a tragedy is often a character's "signature" speech, summing up what is most profoundly characteristic of him. This principle of the signature in the death-speech is particularly clear not only in Shakespeare's tragedies but in *The Duchess of*

Malfi, where everyone who dies says something essential to the understanding of his or her character in the final words. Often in Beddoes, most remarkably in a fragment called *The Last Man,* and again in the last scene with Sibylla in *Death's Jest-Book,* the dramatic action leads up to, or even seems a mere pretext for, a monologue uttered at the point of death. Perhaps Beddoes' real form, so far as it was dramatic, was less the stage play than the kind of near-death monologue represented by Browning's *Bishop Orders His Tomb,* Eliot's *Gerontion,* or Tennyson's *Ulysses.*

We have several times referred to Eliot, whom Beddoes resembles in the way in which he combines a close study of Jacobean dramatists with an ingenuity of imagery that reminds us of Donne and the metaphysicals. Eliot's conception of unified sensibility is really a more complete and flexible version of Beddoes' grotesque. But the pectin, so to speak, that coagulated Eliot's style was a colloquial element derived from French *symboliste* poets and applied to a sense of ironic contrast between a glamorous past and a squalid present. Such an element is related to content: it demands contemporary themes where the presence of the past is part of the irony. One can see Beddoes on the verge of discovering this combination of styles, in some of the deliberately anachronistic passages in the play. But he was too close to the Romantic movement not to adhere in the main to a more conventionally poetic diction: he is even Romantic enough occasionally to distrust the metaphysical and intellectual aspect of his own imagery, and to compare his style, to his own disadvantage, with the true voice of feeling in Shelley. I do not wish to suggest that Beddoes was an Eliot *manqué:* far from it. But he was a poet of brilliant fragments and powerfully suggestive torsos of unfinished plays, and perhaps his genius was pulling him also in the direction of the kind of epic of creative fragmentation represented by *The Waste Land*.

In his dramatic criticism Eliot remarks how the signature speech in Shakespeare, not necessarily the death-speech but any speech in which the character is acting as his own best chorus, like the "tomorrow" speech of Macbeth, throws us more intensely into the dramatic action instead of withdrawing us from it. But although such speeches help to integrate the drama in Shakespeare, they seem to have a tendency to disintegrate it in Beddoes; and even in Eliot himself the detached monologue of Prufrock or Gerontion seems better adapted to the creating of memorable characterization than the more voluntarily constructed stage plays.

In any work of fiction there are two reasons why one episode succeeds another episode. One reason is that it is logically the next episode in the plot: the other is that the author wants it to come next. In most classical dramas which have held the stage there is a plot constructed with sufficient objectivity to enable the dramatist to project his own sense of sequence through it. Such a plot is the "soul" of the action, in Aristotle's phrase, a kind of counter-soul to the poet, and it belongs to an aspect of literature in which the poet is, so to speak, the secretary or recorder of the social process, and is not thinking of his own creative power as itself the center of that process. From the Romantic movement on, the author's desire to have a certain episode come next may be independent of the requirements of the plot; or the plot may disappear in favor of a sequence depending solely on the author's will. This purely thematic, rather than fictional, type of episodic sequence is often rationalized as being like that of a dream, as in Strindberg's *Dream Play,* although the construction of that play is not really dreamlike. Or it may be said to be like that of a pointless and absurd universe, where everything is inconsequential, but this again is a rationalization of the fact that the dramatist wants it that way. In *Death's Jest-Book* one has a feeling that the complex plot is not the inevitable form of what Beddoes has to say, but a separable artefact, and that he did not sufficiently realize that the plot was an obstacle to his dramatic utterance. This is a question of technique which strikes its roots into the center of Romanticism, and we shall return to it in discussing the plotless narratives of Shelley and Keats.

In his characterization, however, as we noted, Beddoes takes a freer hand, and creates not fully realized people, but functional archetypes, that is, characters who illustrate what he has to say rather than what the plot demands that they do. It is natural that the sense of a hidden identity between the inner life of man and the organic processes of nature, the *natura naturans,* should have been accompanied by a good deal of quasi-scientific and pseudo-scientific speculation about the new kinds of knowledge that an apprehension of such an identity would reveal. We noticed in the previous chapter how in "Gothic" fiction many ancient superstitions, the making of homunculi, the conjuring of spirits, vampirism, and the like, took on a new significance as symbolizing the kind of knowledge, whether fascinating or merely sinister, that man might obtain through his renewed contact with the mysteries of nature. Such figures as the mysterious alchemist and mad scientist began to become popular around the end of the eighteenth century, and have continued to be so ever since. The first speaker in *Death's Jest-Book* is Homunculus Mandrake, to whom we have several times referred, who announces that he is going to abandon folly as a profession, thereby rejecting "all sober sense," and pursue wisdom, in such guises as the philosopher's stone and the ointment of invisibility. His studies do not appear to be very fruitful: perhaps this is reflected in the fact that the two lively songs, "Whoever has heard of Saint Gingo" and "Wee, wee tailor," are both parodies of fertility. But still he does illustrate something of Blake's aphorism: "If the fool would persist in his folly he would become wise." The fool in Shakespeare often represents a spirit of mock-logic, presenting plausible arguments and pseudo-syllogisms and paradoxes which his patrons encourage him to "make good." Similarly, Mandrake explains how superstition and the sense of mystery have defined the essentially human quality of folly, and how with the advance of enlightenment, as mystery recedes, each man tends to carry his own death-fool around with him, in the form of a Mephistophelian spirit of denial:

> O world, world! The gods and fairies left thee, for thou wert too wise; and now, thou Socratic star, thy demon, the great Pan, Folly, is parting from thee. The oracles still talked in their sleep, shall our grandchildren say, till Master Merriman's kingdom was broken up: now is every man his own fool, and the world's cheerless.

Other versions of the last three words are: "Fate for us all" and "the world's sign is taken down." Mandrake, a lively person exploring death (his continuous vitality is much insisted on) is a contrast to Ziba the necromancer, who is moving the opposite way, from death to life, and whose crucial act is to raise the avenging spirit of the dead Wolfram.

The Ziba-Mandrake contrast is repeated, on a much larger scale, by the contrast of Wolfram and the Duke. The Duke, Melveric, is a remarkable creation, very like the successful rulers of Shakespeare. He has a deep sense of political responsibility, and has the ruthlessness that goes with success in action. He controls rebellion by a skillful use of disguise and spying, and with the infallible sense of timing that is characteristic of the successful ruler. He is constantly engaged in direct action, but his engagement is at the same time a profound detachment. His is the courage of the born leader who attracts devotion from his followers because he can suggest that he has no need of it, and yet his very self-sufficiency represents something that they profoundly do need. The successful ruler's mind is always inscrutable, but the Duke gives us a hint of the kind of the strength that there is in it:

> *It is this infinite invisible*
> *Which we must learn to know, and yet to scorn,*
> *And, from the scorn of that, regard the world*
> *As from the edge of a far star.*

We almost forget his hideous crimes and watch him sympathetically, feeling that at the end the citizens of Münsterberg are right in preferring him to Isbrand. It is typical of such a man that he should live outside of himself, so to speak, in the present action, avoiding the reflectiveness that turns one to the past or the future. As he says to his son:

> *Think of* now.
> *This Hope and Memory are wild horses, tearing*
> *The precious* now *to pieces.*

It is also typical of a person whose real life is in his actions that whenever he does reflect he should become the blackest of pessimists. As soon as his world is separated from him and becomes objective, it turns into hell. When he reflects, the horror of the past and the nothingness of the future come crowding in on him and annihilate the exuberant rhythm of present action:

> *The look of the world's a lie, a face made up*
> *O'er graves and fiery depths; and nothing's true*
> *But what is horrible.*

And yet at the same time a nihilism of spirit is always with him: this is symbolized by Wolfram's haunting of him. When Wolfram first appears he reacts with great courage, saying that he refuses to believe what is in front of him and threatening to turn Wolfram into "my fool, ghost, my jest and zany," in the tonality of the central death-fool theme. But he is entirely unable to avert Wolfram's appearance, partly because he is already possessed by death.

The heroine Sibylla is first introduced to us as essentially a creation of the Duke's, who has raised her out of prison and given her her first glimpse of her brave new world. He talks of taking her home and bestowing her on some lover destined for her, but as soon as the destined lover turns up in the person of Wolfram, the Duke forgets his generosity and begins to hate Wolfram. The implication is that what he loves is less Sibylla than something in himself that he can make Wolfram a sacrifice to. Later, as mentioned, Sibylla is carried off to the underworld by Wolfram while the Duke turns to seek his own underworld bride, his buried wife, who, being naturally older than Sibylla, is something of a Demeter to her Proserpine. In his brooding over her grave the Duke reminds us a little of the old man in Chaucer's *Pardoner's Tale* who keeps begging his mother Earth to readmit him to her body.

Isbrand is the chief spokesman for the death-fool equation, and, being disguised as a fool, he is, for most of the play, closer to the human sense of the identity of wisdom and folly. He is more reflective than the Duke by temperament, partly because his mind, being engaged in plotting revenge, is thrown forward to the future. Like Poe's

Hop-Frog, he is a jester whose disguise will make possible a revenge which will be an epiphany of death: as he says in one of several passages which associate the tolling of funeral bells with the bells of the fool's cap: "I shall triumph like Jupiter in my fool's cap, to fetch the Duke and his sons to Hell, and then my bells will ring merrily, and I shall jest more merrily than now: for I shall be Death the Court-fool."

His revenge is deflected, however, by his misuse of the success of his political conspiracy against the Duke. Once in power, the cloud of his revenge-anxiety lifts, and he feels in himself the same exhilaration in ruthless action that the Duke felt. Unlike the Duke, however, he tends to intellectualize it in a Nietzschean superman philosophy, dramatizing himself as a self-surpassing hero who is "tired of being no more than human":

> It was ever
> My study to find out a way to godhead,
> And on reflection soon I found that first
> I was but half created; that a power
> Was wanting in my soul to be its soul,
> And this was mine to make. Therefore I fashioned
> A will above my will, that plays upon it,
> As the first soul doth use in men and cattle.

He speaks well and convincingly, but he has lost his sense of irony, and is betraying the essential humanity in himself which his fool's role symbolized. Hence he is falling into the attitude of mind that he hated in the Duke, though without the Duke's sense of detachment about doing a job that he neither likes nor dislikes. Isbrand and the Duke are both quixotic characters, men trying to be angels or gods, and consequently they are arbitrary rulers, pulling away

from the democracy that death the leveler represents. The
link between them is expressed by Isbrand when he speaks
of doing with his ambition what the Duke tried to do with
his wife:

> *The tools I've used*
> *To chisel an old heap of stony laws,*
> *The abandoned sepulchre of a dead dukedom,*
> *Into the form my spirit loved and longed for;*
> *Now that I've perfected her beauteous shape,*
> *And animated it with half my ghost;*
> *Now that I lead her to our bridal bed . . .*

The exceptional person is exceptionally isolated, and
may in himself be a force for exceptional good or evil: as
Isbrand says to himself when plotting revenge:

> *Art thou alone? Why, so should be*
> *Creators and Destroyers.*

But of the three "brothers" (for Wolfram and the Duke
are spoken of as blood-brothers), only Wolfram, with his
gentle and forgiving spirit, so compassionate that he even
refrains from haunting the Duke until compelled to do so,
achieves a genuinely human combination of detachment
and engagement. The interpenetration of life and death,
therefore, so central in Beddoes' imagery, is not quite the
same thing as the interpenetration of good and evil. We
have already referred to the significance of Byron in popu-
larizing a new sense of moral ambiguity: the sense of the
curse of genius, the isolation caused by the possession of
greater powers than ordinary. In Byron this theme is
treated more or less aesthetically: that is, it is seen from a
distance, and we can read about the Corsair's one virtue

and thousand crimes without being troubled by what the characters in *The Playboy of the Western World* felt to be an important distinction after they had experienced both: the distinction between "a gallus story and a dirty deed." This aesthetic approach to the moral complexity of the human situation is reflected in Byron's style. Byron himself was a witty, sociable, extroverted poet of great common sense and (much the same thing) relatively few anxieties, hence it was easy for him to adopt, in *Don Juan,* a persona of detached ironic amusement. At the same time he could project the Byronic hero, as a kind of demonic shadow of himself, into his tales and tragedies, including *Childe Harold*. But to have identified the two would have destroyed his sense of identity, and he never achieved or even attempted the fusion of the two moods in the grotesque as Beddoes did (except perhaps in the last canto of *Don Juan,* and there only on an Ingoldsby-Legends level).

Beddoes' grotesque is thus an inseparable part of a less aesthetic and more existential approach than Byron's, an approach which naturally ensured that he would never be, like Byron, a popular poet. For Beddoes, we are plunged into a world which, in spite of all the violence and irony, is still a world of morally significant choices:

> *I know the moment: 'tis a dreadful one,*
> *Which in the life of every one comes once;*
> *When for the frighted hesitating soul*
> *High heaven and luring sin with promises*
> *Bid and contend.*

This is the Duke talking himself into murdering Wolfram, and it is clear that Beddoes understands what some philosophers of resolute decision and *Augenblick* have not understood: that most resolute decisions are perverse and that a

philosophy founded on the conception of resolute decision
is off its head. The real resolute decision is much more
likely to be a refusal to act rather than an action, like Wolfram's renunciation of revenge. This is a point that we
shall find more fully developed in Shelley, from whom
Beddoes partly derived it.

At the moment when the Duke determines on Wolfram's death he says:

> *Then Amen is said*
> *Unto thy time of being in the world.*

The words "being," "time," and "world" appear together
at least three times in *Death's Jest-Book,* and there are
many passages, here and elsewhere in Beddoes, where we
have one or two of them, along with some synonym of the
others. Being, in Beddoes, refers primarily to an eternity
beyond death, a "great round Ever" or ground of reality
out of which both life and death emerge. What we see, the
'world," we see as we see the moon, with only its lit-up
half turned to us. In *The Second Brother* eternity is described under the figure of the ouroboros, the world-ser-
pent whose tail of death and crown of life meet together,
when the death-figure Marcello meets the life-figure Orazio:

> *Look you, the round earth's sleeping like a serpent*
> *Who drops her dusty tail upon her crown*
> *Just here.*

Eternity, which includes both life and death, is the world
of our full identity. To be born into an individual life and
consciousness is therefore to be thrown into an unbalanced
state, "excepted from eternity," as Sibylla says, and the

proper function of death is to recover the balance. In a figure which goes back as far as the pre-Socratic philosopher Anaximander, one dies to pay the debt to nature incurred by being born, to make "amends" (Sibylla's word) for having been an individual Consciousness, then, is a kind of withdrawal from being, a death-principle which fulfills itself by possessing death. The death-speech of the heroine of the fragmentary *Last Man,* already mentioned, speaks of death as a kind of flight of the alone to the alone, where the individual becomes a universe in himself, a microcosm of the actual universe, and so attains a genuine sense of being at the center of reality:

> *And thou the sum of these, nature of all,*
> *Thou providence pervading the whole space*
> *Of measureless creation; thou vast mind*
>
>   .   .   .
>
> *All hail! I too am an eternity;*
> *I am an universe . . .*
> *'Round and around the curvous atmosphere*
> *Of my own real existence I revolve,*
> *Serene and starry with undying love.*
> *I am, I have been, I shall be, O glory!*
> *An universe, a god, a living Ever.*   [*Dies.*

It appears, then, that birth is a shifting of the center from the universe to the individual ego. To be born is to acquire a lost soul: everybody therefore has a lost soul, and the important thing is to make sure that it gets lost. The crimes, first of the Duke, then of his son Athulf, and the hybris of Isbrand after his revolt, show that they are clinging to this lost soul, and seeking identity through it. Hence, though in one sense they die in the moment of their crimes, in another sense they are really trying to resist the surrendering act of death, trying, once again, to be gods or angels or demons in an egocentric eternity. Wolfram and Sibylla, on the other hand, understand that "It is the earth that falls away from light" (elsewhere "day"), and for them death is the dragon guarding the treasure of identity. For those who achieve that identity, death is the death of death.

Time is what enables being to appear as the world, and the world is eternity so far as we see it extended in space. But time itself is also death and illusion, the power that carries everything away into nothingness. The appearance of time in our world is symbolized in Beddoes, as it so often is in Romantic and modern poets, by a river flowing to the sea of eternity. As the world is what we see of eternity, the rest of eternity, the world of death that we cannot see and so assume to have been annihilated, is mostly the part of it that has been carried away by time. Many of Beddoes' most remarkable images are based on the sense of the liquidness of life, of the living body as a continuous stream which is never the same twice. Athulf says of Amala, for instance:

> *but when she moves, you see,*
> *Like water from a crystal overfilled,*
> *Fresh beauty tremble out of her and lave*
> *Her fair sides to the ground.*

The river reflects the world above it, as the pool did Narcissus, and the preoccupation of life with death is symbolized by reflection and mirrors. Thus it is said of knights in armor that their "shields, like water, glassed the soul-eyed maidens." Echoes of the Biblical deluge and of the Red Sea that hungers for ghosts, referred to by Mandrake at the beginning of the play, usually linger around such passages. In one extraordinary fragment, beginning "And many voices marshalled in one hymn," there appears to be an association between the vision of eternity and the Israelites moving through the sea. The contrasting images are those of mountains, towers, and rocks that stand in the sea and refuse to be dissolved: they represent the kind of criminal titanism that tries to escape from the surrender of death by recklessness and despair. Thus Athulf, after he murders his brother, feels like "a wild old wicked mountain in the sea," and the Duke is told that for his murder of Wolfram:

> *like an old, haunted mountain,*
> *Icy and hoary, shalt thou stand 'mid life.*

Similarly, the common Romantic image of the boat tossing on water is linked by Beddoes with life journeying to its ultimate fulfillment through death. Sibylla links the image of the resisting mountain to a Lohengrin-like picture of her ghost-lover:

> *Speak as at first you did; there was in the words*
> *A mystery and music, which did thaw*
> *The hard old rocky world into a flood,*
> *Whereon a swan-drawn boat seemed at my feet*
> *Rocking on its blue billows.*

The "world," of course, as already said, is the visible or spatial world which conceals a dark invisible world on the side turned away from us, the kingdom of the black sun beyond. Long before we rejoin it we are aware of the influence of the death-world on us. It seeps into our lives in the form of sleep and dream, and brings a refreshment and strengthening to us in a way that suggests that it is something considerably more than a mere negation. Sibylla says after a night's sleep:

> *Deeply have I slept.*
> *As one who doth go down unto the springs*
> *Of his existence and there bathed, I come*
> *Regenerate up into the world again.*

This takes us back to the traditional image of the underground oracle, as well as to the *Kubla Khan* imagery of subterranean rivers. The world of sleep and dream is thus also the world from which the poet and the prophet draw their revelations, the poet being in our day the chief transmitter of "the prophecies"

> *which flicker up*
> *Out of the sun's grave underneath the world.*

Hence the poet is typically in the position of Wolfram, or of Samuel in the Witch of Endor story, who has kept a communication line open to this lower world. In another poem Beddoes thus describes a poet:

> *the truth was restless in him,*
> *And shook his visionary fabrics down,*
> *As one who had been buried long ago*
> *And now was called up by a necromancer*
> *To answer dreadful questions.*

The voice of this buried world has the peculiarly ambivalent quality of the grotesque: it is at once oracular and witty, inspiring awe and yet provoking the laughter of the intelligence. Strange rumors come to us from this world, rumors of some indefinitely repeated process going on in both nature and human life, of rebirth and reincarnation, of man's present body as a seed of the tree of ghosts, of dreams as the spirits of the dead living in us.

Simple and primitive societies, one character in the play suggests, are more apt to be haunted by the dead because the dead of such societies are lonely, and make their way back to a community of greater cheerfulness. As time goes on the dead become the majority—*migravit ad plures* was a stock phrase about one recently dead—and great cities have been formed in the dead world, so we may expect that "There will be no more haunting." In proportion as death has become populous, it has become the past of which our own knowledge is a recollection. It is the realm of the permanent achievements of mankind, which are not lost in time as they appear to be, but are simply carried away by time. Thus the world of death acquires through time a kind of moral stability which helps to balance our own lives.

It is an old assumption of tragedy that time—that is, death—will discover crimes and that revenge may come through ghosts. In ordinary life conscience and remorse are evidence of the permanence of what has been done in the vanished past: of conscience Isbrand says that it "doth prattle with the voices of the dead through the speaking trumpet of the winds." Similarly, a man may conceal a crime from the world of the living, as the Duke did his murder of Wolfram, but such a crime makes one visible to the world of the dead, hence the tradition of murderers being haunted by their victims. Athulf, after his murder of his brother, understands how a "mortal" sin is in fact a death of the soul, killing the sinner without making any apparent change in his status:

I am unsouled, dishumanized, uncreated;
My passions swell and grow like brutes conceived

.   .   .

I break, and magnify, and lose my form.
And yet I shall be taken for a man,
And never be discovered till I die.

This is the end, for Athulf, of what we have been calling angelism, the attempt to dominate one's world by a self-transcending will instead of admitting one's limitations, and so persisting in folly. Wolfram, who suffers but does not inflict injustice, is emancipated into the world of pure death: Isbrand, because he is vowed to conspiracy and revenge, acts as a nemesis or agent of dark unseen forces that are nevertheless on the side of a kind of rough justice in human affairs. Revolutions may also be uprisings of the same hidden force which makes for a renewed order, and are described, as is Isbrand's revenge, in the imagery of volcanoes and earthquakes, an energy pushing up from below.

A question has already arisen: if death so interpenetrates with life, and if there is such variety of good and evil in life, is there any variety in death as well? Death seems too unvarying a category to be more than accidentally connected with life. It is alike the punishment of the villain and the reward of his victim, the end of revenge on Melveric and the release of Sibylla. Beddoes, who is not working out his poems within any definite structure of doctrine, religious or otherwise, does not give a very clear answer to this. But it does seem that there is some difference between death and deadness. Of Wolfram, Sibylla says (notice the three words again, with "motion" substituted for "time"):

This utterance and token of his being
His spirit hath let fall, and now is gone
To fill up nature and complete her being.
The form, that here is fallen, was the engine,
Which drew a great motion of spiritual power
Out of the world's own soul, and made it play
In visible motion, as the lofty tower
Leads down the animating fire of heaven
To the world's use.

For Wolfram, therefore, death seems to be a reintegration. But the deadness of spirit that the Duke intermittently feels is rather a feeling of being cut off:

I do begin to feel
As if I were a ghost among the men,
As all I loved are; for their affections
Hang on things new, young, and unknown to me:
And that I am is but the obstinate will
Of this my hostile body.

The play ends with the identity of life and death expressed in its most complete antithesis. Wolfram is a ghost who has unwillingly come back into life, bringing with him the love and the justice that proceed from the invisible world; the Duke is a living man who is at the same time eternally dead, and who, like the Wandering Jew, cannot find the peace of real death. To the ignorant, death is solemn, the king of terrors; for the Duke, it is a repose denied him; to Wolfram, it is the supreme joke, the sudden emergence of what we ordinarily keep repressed and yet know to be really there. It is a practical joke in bad taste, like Yorick's practical joke on the grave-digger, but it establishes the limits of what is human, and makes those who attempt the inhuman, the subhuman, or, like Isbrand, the superhuman, look like unsuccessful fools.

What Beddoes contributes to Romanticism is, perhaps, the most complete and searching poetic reaction to the Romantic sense of the limitations of ordinary experience. The shadow of Kant's riddle falls across the whole Romantic movement. The world that we see and understand is not the noumenon, the world in itself, but only the world as phenomenon, as adapted to our categories of perception and reasoning. The inference is that *real* reality, so to speak, cannot be known, at least not by the subject-object relationship. The proud boast of the subjective reason, that a perfect being must exist because the mind can conceive the possibility of its existence, no longer carries much conviction. The Romantic sense of something outside ordinary experience which nevertheless completes experience, symbolized by "nature" in Wordsworth and elsewhere, must be something mysterious, because it cannot be directly apprehended. It is obvious that the Kantian distinction affords a justification for imaginative, as distinct from rational, knowledge, and for symbolism. The phenomenon, which represents a reality that it does not exhaust, is a symbol of what is really there, but it is a fixed and invariable symbol, perceived involuntarily and unalterable as a perception. Poetry creates for the imagination a flexible language of symbols, and expands our range of experience accordingly, in a way that sense and reason cannot do.

On this basis, various poetic and philosophical reactions to the Kantian position are possible. For some, the noumenal world is a world of mystical identity. I know the table I write on as a phenomenon, but if I could know the table as it really is in itself I would be that table. For others, we are related to the noumenal world by our existence, and we experience noumenal reality through the engagements of our existence. For Carlyle, more specifically, the noumenal world is the naked world under the clothes of phenomena which both conceal it and reveal it. But Beddoes, identifying this invisible and underlying reality with death, seems, if I may put it so, to have hit a bullseye that many of his contemporaries saw but tried not to hit. He anticipates later preoccupations with the relation of being and nothingness more directly than most Romantics. When Sartre tells us that man essentially is, not what he has done, but what he is about to make of himself, his life thus moving onward to an identity which can be reached only by death, he is formulating the same kind of paradox as Beddoes. The feeling that the moment of death is also a crisis of identity is probably as old as human consciousness, and certainly as old as written literature. But it starts out on a new and lonelier journey with the Romantic movement, a journey with a continuous sense that, as Eliot says, the moment of death is every moment, and that absurdity is the only visible form of the meaning of life. It is Beddoes, as far as English literature is concerned, who brings us most directly into contact with the conception of the absurd in a way that permits of compassion but excludes self-pity.

Prometheus:

The Romantic Revolutionary

We have isolated one element in the Romantic revolution as the recovery by man of a good deal of what he formerly projected on God. Creative power, the desire for liberty, and the capacity to make myths and to design the structures of civilization are increasingly regarded as originating in the human mind. One would expect, then, the growth of a secular humanism in poetry, where man is seen as building a better world for himself out of his own resources. Central among these resources would be science, man's new direct knowledge of his environment, and technology, his even newer ability to apply it. We do in fact get a certain amount of such literature, mainly in France, where the social effects of the French Revolution naturally centered. But we noted that there seems to have been, since the Romantic movement at least, a persistent separation of the scientific vision of nature, the informing language of which becomes increasingly mathematical rather than verbal, from the existential myth to which the poetic vision belongs. Poetry speaks, not the language of fact or reason, but the language of concern, of hopes and fears and desires and hatreds and dreams. Poets frequently announce that they are about to make a functional use of contemporary science and technology and get into the modern world, but the tolerance of poetry for this kind of language seems to be limited.

If any poet in English literature could have used the language and conceptions of science successfully, it would surely have been Shelley. An unusual sense of nature as subject to law and orderly process, a precision of imagery (when he wanted to be precise), and a command of abstract and philosophical language are among his obvious qualities. Furthermore, one of his earliest intuitions was that the idea of a personal God, considered as creator of both man and the natural environment, was a notion projected from, and thereby perverting, the creative power of the human mind. Man is a myth-making as well as a tool-using animal, but constant vigilance is needed to make sure that he keeps control of what he makes. For it is with myths as it is with technology: just as man invents the wheel and then talks about a wheel of fate or fortune overriding everything he does, so he creates gods and then announces that the gods have created him. He makes his own creation, in short, a power to stop himself from creating.

In *The Revolt of Islam* some sailors, agents of a tyrant, have abducted the heroine, who, doubtless estimating their intentions correctly, breaks into a harangue which covers most of the eighth canto, in which she explains how the conception of God arose from projection:

> *What is that Power? Some moon-struck sophist stood*
> *Watching the shade from his own soul upthrown*
> *Fill Heaven and darken Earth, and in such mood*
> *The Form he saw and worshipped was his own,*
> *His likeness in the world's vast mirror shown.*

Once they understand this, she remarks pointedly, their attitudes toward a number of other things will also change:

> *Know yourselves thus! ye shall be pure as dew,*
> *And I will be a friend and sister unto you.*

In any case, a poet who devotes himself, as Shelley did, not merely to mythopoeic poetry but specifically to man's recovery of his own myth-making powers, is bound to find his mythology consolidating on the figure of Prometheus, whose name traditionally means imagination ("forethought"), and who was martyred by the gods for his friendship to man. Similarly, Prometheus' deliverance is achieved when the projected Jupiter falls back into the cave of myths whence he originated, and becomes identical with his phantasm, in accordance with Prometheus' remark to the phantasm:

> *as thou art must be*
> *He whom thou shadowest forth.*

It is not surprising that Shelley's first major effort, *Queen Mab,* should be in large part an essay in versified scientism, celebrating the superseding of religion by a more rational and secular attitude.

Yet *Queen Mab* is so obviously not on the direct path of Shelley's poetic development that we have to look further than the mere immaturity of the poem itself for the reasons. A personal God, it is true, has no status in the scientific vision: he is replaced by natural law, and natural law operates most freely in the world of the dead or inanimate. In the world of time and space, then, God is dead: he was of course never alive there, but any God who can die is much better dead. But what we are then left with is the scientific vision of law, in which the human mind confronts a subhuman world. It is in the realm of the automatic and predictable that science moves with most assurance, but human beings themselves clearly belong, at least in large part, to a different realm, and we can perceive nothing externally that is, to put it crudely, any better than we are. We may gain intuitions of a superhuman process which unites us with nature, but we do not perceive any such process as a conscious subject. What we perceive, or rather infer from what we perceive, is what *Queen Mab,* quite logically and consistently, leads up to: a vision of "Nature's [elsewhere "Necessity's"] unchanging harmony."

But this gives us a view of the human situation which is very like an extremely rigorous Christian view, with nature substituted for God. Nature forms a harmonious order from which man alone is excluded. Man in his present state is the scapegoat or *pharmakos* of nature, the only unnatural being, and nothing can help him except reconciliation with nature. Nature's gospel is nature's law, which when accepted becomes freedom as well as necessity. As with more conventional creeds, the difficulty and complexity of regeneration is got around by being transferred to an anxiety-symbol which substitutes for it. The eating of meat occupies the same place in Shelley's poem that similar fetishes do in institutional religion. Prometheus enters the footnotes to

Queen Mab, where it is said that he "represents the human race," but where he is bound down on the stems of vegetarianism, to misquote Blake. His theft of fire is said to symbolize the original sin of cooking meat, which, as the myth explains, turned out to be very bad for his liver.

Queen Mab is going in the direction, not of a fuller humanism, but of what Blake calls "natural religion," a faith with necessity and law substituted for the will of a personal God, which would have all the fanaticism and intolerance of its Christian predecessor without any of the loopholes for the imagination that Christianity at its worst still provided. It would be, in the imagery of *Prometheus Unbound,* Jupiter made omnipotent by marriage to Thetis, whose name perhaps connects with ideas of the prescribed and ordained. One arrives at this sort of godless religion by maintaining the supremacy of the rational, or subject-object, view of the world. God, conceived as the creator of the natural order that we look at, vanishes into Necessity as soon as we do look at it. "The necessity of atheism," the subject of Shelley's earliest metaphysical speculation, takes us only as far as an atheism of necessity.

The next step for Shelley was to relegate the subject-object view to a secondary position in the mind and incorporate it into a poetic or imaginative view. Philosophically, this step is associated by Shelley with a change from materialism, or whatever *Queen Mab* expounded, to the subjective idealism of Berkeley. Necessity's unchanging harmony may be regarded as the irreducible minimum of the human condition, the sense of order and regularity which is the foundation of life. It is, in Blake's phrase, a starry floor, not a ceiling. For a creative consciousness to identify the limit of its development with something essentially mindless would be the most pointless of self-humiliations. The vision of law in the external world is only part of a much larger vision. This larger vision is based, not on what we see and understand, but on what we want and do not want. It has two poles, a positive pole of desire, the vision of what man wishes to become, and a negative pole of repugnance, the vision of what man wants to escape from or annihilate.

The positive pole is represented in Shelley chiefly by images of incredibly swift movement through air or water, often on "cars" or vehicles equipped with the symbolic equivalent of an internal combustion engine. There is something here that we notice elsewhere in Romanticism, a change in human sensibility which takes the form of an altering of proportions. Especially in America, cities and the settled countryside take on an increasingly geometrical form, and we realize that the visible form of civilization is changing from a proportion related to the human body to a proportion related to the mechanical extensions of the body. In Romantic music and poetry we begin to notice an inner propulsion that has something mechanical in it— though we must be careful not to use this word, in a metaphor popularized by Romanticism itself, as a merely pejorative term. This kind of propulsion comes into Wordsworth's *Idiot Boy, Peter Bell,* and *The Waggoner,* where we hear a good deal about flying boats. As the thief of fire, Prometheus of course has a technological side, and the sense that a rapidly stepped-up conquest of space is not far off in human destiny lurks in such poems as *The Witch of Atlas,* to say nothing of *Prometheus Unbound* itself. We understand Shelley very well when he says:

> *Whoever should behold me now, I wist,*
> *Would think I were a mighty mechanist,*
> *Bent with sublime Archimedean art*
> *To breathe a soul into the iron heart*

Of some machine portentous, or strange gin,
Which by the force of figured spells might win
Its way over the sea, and sport therein.

However, we should expect to find most Romantic poets very cautious, if not openly hostile, in their approach to such themes. Blake, for instance, uses a good deal of mechanical and technological imagery, but he emphasizes the sinister side of it: its connection with exploitation and alienation, its development of improved ways of killing people in vast numbers, its role in reinforcing brutally repressive regimes. An awareness of the same general kind, which, if not sinister, is at least extremely ambiguous, comes into De Quincey's powerful essay *The English Mail-Coach*. The mail-coach is part of a big spider-web of a central intelligence, a new kind of personality which is at once human and mechanical. As that it is partly demonic, a Juggernaut with a baleful dragon-eye, bearing news of victory and of death, which nearly crushes a helpless young couple, and stirs up in the poet the central anxiety-dream, the dream which repeats the original fall of man.

The sense of the new technology as demonic is connected with the sense of its aggressiveness. Man allies himself with the dead and mechanical in order to attack and conquer nature, which he is still thinking of as objective, as set over against him. It is not set over against him, however, but is part of himself, hence he is engaging in his old projecting game of enslaving himself to what he creates. Or, as Shelley says, "man, having enslaved the elements, remains himself a slave." The automotive boats and unidentified flying objects in Shelley, on the other hand, represent rather a physical and mental identity with nature, where space is receding because the human mind and its powers are expanding. The swift vehicles are symbols of desire,

and are swift because human emotions are swift: as the
Spirit of the Hour says of his "coursers":

> *I desire: and their speed makes night kindle;*
> *I fear: they outstrip the Typhoon.*

The same feeling comes into Shelley's natural imagery as
well. In *The Cloud,* to take a familiar example, we feel that
we ourselves are riding on the cycle of nature, participating in what might better be called its changing harmony;
and similarly with the loving description in *Prometheus
Unbound* of the spirits of the elements riding up through
the water in bubbles and then going back again to repeat
the process.

We notice that in painting, as well as in poetry, a new
sense of man's relation to nature is developing. With Rembrandt, painting reflects a culture in which the subject-object relation is primary: in his pictures we are looking at an
objective order. Coleridge's conception of the artist imitating
nature by identifying himself with the *natura naturans* or
living process of nature, which we referred to in the first
chapter, is implicit in his remarks on the painting of
Washington Allston. The remarks have little to do with
Allston, but, considered in connection with painting, have a
good deal to do with the pictorial development which began with late Turner and carried on through the Impres-
sionists. In such painting we are still in the area of repre-
sentation, even of "realism," but it is a realism that renders
a sense of rhythm and movement in nature, and that demands a physical sense of participating in this rhythm from
us. In some of Shelley's color fantasies something of the
pictorial feeling of late Turner is anticipated:

The point of one white star is quivering still
Deep in the orange light of widening morn
Beyond the purple mountains: through a chasm
Of wind-divided mist the darker lake
Reflects it: now it wanes: it gleams again
As the waves fade, and as the burning threads
Of woven cloud unravel in pale air:
'Tis lost! and through yon peaks of cloud-like snow
The roseate sunlight quivers: hear I not
The Aeolian music of her sea-green plumes
Winnowing the crimson dawn?

The negative or ironic pole of the poetic vision is the sense of nature as objective and separated from the consciousness, but looked at by the consciousness in the light of imagination and desire and not of reason. Seen by the reason as an objective order, nature makes rational sense. Seen by imagination, creativity, and desire, it makes no sense at all. It presents us with an endless expanse of mindlessness: where it is alive it is cruel; where it is dead it is empty. It presents us, therefore, with the sense of the anguished and the absurd. This is the inevitable consequence, for Shelley, of dropping the projected God of nature, and is foreshadowed in the notes to *Queen Mab*: "But if the principle of the universe be not an organic being, the model and prototype of man, the relation between it and human beings is absolutely none."

In *Prometheus Unbound* we have again what we had in *Queen Mab,* man as the scapegoat of nature, the only power that resists Jupiter. But Shelley has reversed his earlier notion of seeking reconciliation with Jupiter. Prometheus is now the human mind confronting the objective world with its own desire, and Jupiter is the mental block which prevents man from trying to conceive and reshape a world beyond that order. The reason that man clings to the notion of a personal God in nature as an objective counterpart of himself is that, once this deity goes, he then confronts a moral chaos, an absurdity. To be aware of the creation, as it now is, is to be aware of anguish. In the notes to *Queen Mab* there occurs the extraordinary phrase, "The supereminence of man is like Satan's, a supereminence of pain," and this is especially true of Prometheus. Yet pain is the condition which keeps Prometheus conscious, and consciousness is the only power that can be a threat to Jupiter. If man could lose his specifically human consciousness, he would also lose his specifically human pain and misery; but it would be a poor exchange.

Prometheus Unbound is based on two contrasting visions of nature. The Jupiter death-vision is the objective order perceived by what is in every sense of the word a subject. The source of all error in religion is the notion that this external order is a "creation." What it is is our own creation in a degenerate form. Through automatic and unquestioning habit, what we repeatedly see becomes familiar, and in proportion as it becomes familiar, the counterpart of what perceives it, it becomes first separate, then indifferent, then mindless, and finally a chaos. Genuine creation, or poetry, "creates anew the universe, after it has been annihilated in our minds by the recurrence of impressions blunted by reiteration," as Shelley says in *The Defence of Poetry*. The fact that Jupiter's real impetus is toward chaos rather than order comes out in the moment of his fall:

> *Let hell unlock*
> *Its mounded oceans of tempestuous fire,*

And whelm on them into the bottomless void
This desolated world, and thee, and me.

The human society of ordinary experience is a part of the Jupiter vision: it is founded on all the things we see in nature, cruelty, repression, the domination of evil will, and above all the inertia of habit, which appears in society as custom, the unthinking acceptance of what is there because it is there. Jupiter is inertia deified, and unites a submissive attitude to nature with a submissive social attitude, in which the symbolic bogies of Shelley, the King and Priest, arise because even degenerate Nature will not tolerate a vacuum. In Shelley, as in all revolutionary Romantics, society is liberated through the agency of another aspect of nature, the aspect we have associated with the sublime in the later eighteenth century; with participation in the power that links us to nature in Wordsworth; with the myth of Esau or Ishmael, the exiled and wandering but rightful heir, in Byronic fiction; and, later, with the world of the dead in Beddoes. We have now to see what its associations are in Shelley.

Prometheus Unbound is a comedy in the sense that it ends happily with the freeing of the hero and the accompanying festivities of a new human order. In comedy the hero's love for the heroine normally wins out over the sinister and ridiculous characters who try to thwart it, of which the central one is usually a father-figure. Shelley's Jupiter, like the *senex* of so many comedies, has his own sexual ambitions, designed to annihilate those of the hero, but he is baffled in the moment of his apparent triumph. The imagery of *Prometheus Unbound* is of course not that of any comedy of manners, but it has some affinities with Shakespeare's romantic comedies. Shakespearean comedy, we said, begins with a world presented as a world of ordinary experience, often a court, with repressive characteristics usually attached to it. This world collides with another world associated with sleep, dream, magic, fairies, sexual desire, and a more direct contact with a physical nature unspoiled by human perversity. I call the latter world in Shakespeare, because it is so often a forest or pastoral landscape, the "green world," a phrase occurring in both *Prometheus Unbound* and *Endymion* (Beddoes, whose diction is habitually more abstract, speaks of "the green creation" in *The Bride's Tragedy*). The victory of the green world in the comic action indicates that desire and love are not merely impotent expressions of a "pleasure principle" feebly struggling against reality, as in Freud, but mighty powers capable of subduing reality to themselves.

Two features of Shakespearean comedy are particularly relevant to Shelley. First: in the traditional schema, unfallen nature, both human and physical, possesses a harmony which the nature we know has lost. This harmony is symbolized by the music of the spheres. The spheres of the planets are, in many versions of the Ptolemaic cosmos, guided by angelic intelligences. Below the lowest planet, the moon, comes the world of the four elements. These elements, of course, have no angels, but there are, in poetry and in some speculative thought, elemental spirits, who may be controlled by magic. As an art, magic, in poetry, symbolizes the regaining of a lost rapport with the "sublunary" part of the physical world, assuming that the magic is morally benevolent. In *A Midsummer Night's Dream* the fairies are expressly said to be spirits of the elements, whose dissension causes bad weather. Yet they are able to intervene in the actions of human beings too, their influence being in the direction of promoting true love and evading the harsh *senex*-centered laws of Athens.

In *The Tempest* an entire society is recreated by Prospero's magic into a higher order of nature, largely through the agency of elemental spirits, Ariel in particular. What began as a shipwrecked group of clowns and gangsters in which "no man was his own" ends in a brave new world, a society with its original structure intact, but permeated by a spirit of reconciliation. Shakespeare, however, is (at least in *The Tempest*) working with the older schema in which the higher level of nature is purely human. Ariel, not being human, cannot enter such a world, and has to be left to be free in his own element. In *Prometheus Unbound* there are a great many spirits, and a number of them are expressly connected with the elements. But in Shelley's Romantic cosmos there is no higher human order of nature from which Ariel is excluded. For Shelley the liberation of man and the liberation of nature are different aspects of the same thing, and emancipated man finds himself in a world of emancipated spirits whose poetic originals are clearly Ariel and Puck.

Second: the green world of Shakespeare is a Dionysian world, a world of energy and exuberance. Even in some of the tragedies there is a similar kind of world, though in tragedy it loses out to its narrower and harsher rival. In *Romeo and Juliet,* for example, the world of Queen Mab's dreams, the passion of the lovers, and the wild energy of Juliet's speech to the night are destroyed by the daylight feud, and in *Antony and Cleopatra* Mark Antony's extravagant vitality is contrasted with the calculated discipline of Rome, which in a tragic situation is certain to defeat it. Shelley's use of "Queen Mab" as a title for his first long poem indicates his affinity with this theme in Shakespeare, however little use he makes of Queen Mab herself. In *Prometheus Unbound* the green world is not only a world of elemental spirits, but is explicitly Dionysian: the

two "fauns" who watch the spirits playing like the released Ariel are followers of Silenus, and the entire drama
gives us the sense of a prodigious repressed "enthusiasm"
in nature, in the literal sense of a Dionysian divine presence, which is impatiently awaiting the signal of release.

In comedy, again, the absurd or tyrannical characters
who block the hero's marriage are upsetting the social
order which the audience sees to be the right and proper
one. Consequently, the comic action leads to a restoration
of that order, which may be thought of as hypothetical or as
preceding the action of the play. Similarly, the victory won
by Prometheus over Jupiter is a victory over the kind of
religion now associated with the names of Jehovah and
Jesus, and a restoration of many of the elements of pre-
Christian Greek culture. For Shelley, the canon of imaginative revelation was Greek rather than Hebrew. In a draft
of *The Defence of Poetry* he says of the century preceding
the death of Socrates: "It is as if the continent of Paradise
were overwhelmed and some shattered crag remained cov-
ered with asphodel and amaranth which bear a golden
flower." The phraseology transfers to Greece the orthodox
Christian beliefs about the originality of Hebrew and Biblical traditions. We can see in many German Romantics how,
as soon as the Christian Creator of nature begins to fade
into projection, the Greek gods leap into an almost obsessive
vitality, not as gods, but as images of a *human* wholeness and
spontaneity which has been destroyed by self-consciousness.
Shelley is the closest of all English poets to this "tyranny
of Greece," as it has been called. Greek religion for Shelley
was more flexible and less pedantic in imposing belief; it
preserved the intuitive sense of identity with natural forces;
its polytheism enabled the scientific and philosophical
views of the world to develop independently. The climax of
Greek culture, the age of Pericles, brought with it a belief

in liberty, not, like the age of the New Testament, a belief in the necessity of submission to tyranny. The prospect of the political independence of Greece from Turkey thus seemed to Shelley to be a genuine form of the crusade, and it stirred up speculations in him about the world's great age beginning anew. The Wandering Jew, who enters *Queen Mab* and re-enters *Hellas,* is a symbol for Shelley of man enduring the tyranny of God until a better era dawns. For, according to *Queen Mab,* the Wandering Jew was cursed out of pure malice by a Christ who was only pretending to suffer on the cross.

Here we touch on the feature of Shelley's thought that so delighted Yeats, the prophecy of a new religion "antithetical" to Christianity and reverting to many features of Greek thought and culture. Shelley's version of this new culture is, to speak plainly, much less vulgar than Yeats': it does not rest on a facile cyclicism or rationalize everything brutal and degenerate in both Greek and modern culture as part of a "tragic" or "heroic" way of life that is to be reintroduced, for Yeats, by fascism. But still there are points in common, and Yeats was doubtless right in seeing in Shelley's Prince Athanase ("immortal"), with his mother and mysterious father, his tragic sense of life, and his courageous loyalty to the destroyed pagan faith, an aesthetic and "antithetical" counterpart to Christ, the tower under the moonrise being the antithesis of the cross under the sunset. Prince Athanase's literary ancestor is, as Yeats says, the pensive Platonist of Milton, reading Greek tragedies, pondering over what spirits, whether of the elements or not, may transcend the Christian cosmos, and eventually adopting a purely aesthetic religion of organ music and stained glass windows. Milton, naturally, drew his *penseroso* figure as the creature of a mood, not as the creator of reality, but for Romanticism both *penseroso* and *allegro* narrators create the worlds they are in, instead of merely responding to them, and hence are something much more significant than mere "humors." We shall meet this point again in Keats.

In the original myth Prometheus was crucified by Zeus for not revealing a secret he held: that Zeus by marriage to Thetis would beget a son greater than himself. Eventually Prometheus did reveal the secret, was released, and Thetis was married off to a mortal, Peleus, their son being Achilles, who, as a warrior, was an agent of, not a threat to, Zeus' tyranny. In Shelley Jupiter announces the begetting of a Son who will make him omnipotent: the scene is intended to recall the parallel announcement by God the Father in the fifth book of *Paradise Lost,* along with its demonic counterpart, Satan's begetting of Death on a female Sin in the second. In the Christian myth, as Shelley reads it, the Father "redeems" man, that is, completes his ascendancy over him, by sending his Son to earth as a spy in disguise:

> *Veiling his horrible Godhead in the shape*
> *Of man.*

From this pair proceeds a "Spirit" who dwells with man and helps to prevent him from doing anything dangerous. If we start with the real starting point for Shelley, man on the earth, this Christian Trinitarian myth goes into reverse.

According to the notes to *Queen Mab,* there is no "creative Deity," but "The hypothesis of a pervading Spirit coeternal with the universe remains unshaken." That is, the name God may legitimately be applied to whatever it is that identifies man and nature in a participating unity. This Spirit is the "Daemon of the World" of the salvaged portion of *Queen Mab,* and he enters *Prometheus Unbound* as Demogorgon. When Demogorgon rises from his cave he is transformed from a Spirit into a risen Son of Jupiter. Evidently the Son proceeds from the Spirit, not the other way round. But Demogorgon, in Yeatsian language, adopts the "antithetical" role of an Oedipus who destroys his father, not that of a "primary" Christ who obeys him. He is the successful Lucifer, the dispossessed elder son, who takes Jupiter back to the human imagination that gave birth to him.

The starting point of most Romantic imagery about the spirit of the world or nature with whom man identifies himself is the speech of the Erdgeist near the beginning of Goethe's *Faust*. The Attendant Spirit of *Comus,* however, who comes from a higher region in an earlier structure of symbolism, also echoes through this speech of a Spirit in Shelley's unfinished drama:

> *Within the silent centre of the earth*
> *My mansion is; where I have lived insphered*
> *From the beginning, and around my sleep*
> *Have woven all the wondrous imagery*
> *Of this dim spot, which mortals call the world.*

If life is the dream of the Earth-Spirit, the poet is the interpreter of that dream, who creates for us a version of the world which is much closer to reality than the world we see. Unity with the Earth-Spirit is the primary or existential identity of man; poetry creates a secondary identity which has, in the words of the Preface to *Prometheus Unbound,* "some intelligible and beautiful analogy with those sources of emotion and thought." The vision of reality which emerges from the caves of the imagination in dreams, oracles, prophecies, and poems seems to us, from the point of view of ordinary, or Jupiter-dominated, experience, a futile and hopeless shadow-world, a Hades of gibbering blood-less bats. But that, in turn, is what our world is like from its point of view. According to the allegory of the cave in Plato, it is in ordinary experience that we find ourselves staring at the flickering shadows of an objective world which is the underworld of reality.

The traditional Christian virtues are faith, hope, and love: of these, faith is the primary virtue, the response to God which enables the other two to develop. Love is the greatest of the virtues, and Christian love is love in the sense of *agape* or *caritas,* man's reproduction of the love that God has for him. In Shelley hope and love retain their place, but his refusal to regard faith as a virtue leads to some uneasy triads: we have "Love, Hope and Self-esteem" in the *Hymn to Intellectual Beauty* and "Hope, Love and Power" in *Prometheus Unbound.* For Shelley, love is the primary virtue, and it begins in the human soul. It is therefore, as mentioned, love in the sense of *eros,* the love of Plato's *Symposium* and Dante's *Vita Nuova,* a human love founded on the sexual instinct. The virtues in Shelley travel in the opposite direction from Christianity: virtue begins in love and flows through hope into whatever Shelley's equivalent of faith is.

Love still has for Shelley a great deal of its earlier speculative associations with attraction, an association still preserved in our word "like." "Like" is the sign of analogy, and analogy is a weakened form of the identity which is the fulfillment of love. "Love makes all things equal," which means, not that it makes everything uniform, but that it is the power of creating unity out of the disparate and divided. In *Epipsychidion* the union of lover and be-loved identifies them into one person, and this union in its turn is the matrix of the genuine creation concealed within the chaos of ordinary experience. With the release of Prometheus this creation reappears, from "its chaos made calm by love, not fear," and man assumes the traditional power of the creator to command the chaos and "walk upon the sea." We call the poet creative because poetry is the real form of the creative word formerly projected on Christ. The language of love is the imaginative language of the poet, and the imagination is, in the words of the Preface to *The Cenci*: "the immortal God which should assume flesh for the redemption of mortal passion." The aesthetic preference of unity to multiplicity which we find in great philosophers, notably Plato, is not a merely intellectual preference, but the preference of the creation of love over the disintegration achieved by fear.

There are books which explain the difference between Plato's *eros* and Paul's *agape,* but unfortunately there is only one Greek word for hope, *elpis,* which covers both the hope of St. Paul and the hope at the bottom of Pandora's box in Hesiod. The studies of *eros* and *agape* seem to have no counterpart, except by implication, in studies of *elpis* and *elpis* prime, yet the hope which proceeds from human love is clearly different from the hope which proceeds from faith in God. A hope based on human love becomes a future-directed hope for the earthly and social regeneration of all mankind. In theory, this belongs to Christian hope too, but in practice Christian hope tends to become centered on the individual's hope for his own future life in Christ, and hence to become restricted to a hope primarily for the people of God. The petition to bring the Kingdom of God on earth remains in the Lord's Prayer, but serious attention to it tends to be regarded as a somewhat pagan and secular hope, based on illusions of "perfectibility" and going too far beyond the perfectly proper hope of converting everybody to the Christian faith. Shelley's future-directed hope for a transcendence of the human condition on earth may be illusory, but it is the same in kind as the revolutionary hope which has proved since his day to be immensely stronger than Christianity. The view taken of Christ in *Prometheus Unbound* is much more charitable than that in *Queen Mab*: in the later poem Jesus is a saintly teacher of humanity whom the mob of Jupiter not only put to death, but destroyed more effectually by annexing his teachings to the Jupiter vision. Even so, of course, this view makes the crucified Christ a type of Prometheus, in contrast to the view of Christianity in which Prometheus would be a type of Christ.

What is Shelley's equivalent of faith? Clearly it is, as our first chapter has suggested, some form of gnosis. At first this gnosis is a secret, perilous and forbidden knowledge, like that of Adam in Eden, snatched from under the nose of a jealous Jupiter, and transmitted through the murmuring oracular caverns of the human poetic imagination. Such knowledge, though secretly acquired, is extremely simple in content, being the message of love that comes through hope. According to the argument of *Prometheus Unbound,* Prometheus loves and is loved, and his hope is unbreakable, hence he is bound to triumph in time. But when he withdraws the curse on Jupiter, his knowledge and will to endure are transformed into a vision that fulfills knowledge and makes further endurance needless. This attainment of vision corresponds in Shelley to the miraculous transformation that, in Christianity, grace makes in the human will.

In *Paradise Lost,* an epic poem of heroic action, Milton had to decide what, in Christian terms, a hero was and what an act was. All acts, according to Milton, are good; Adam's disobedience and Satan's rebellion are therefore not acts but pseudo-acts or parody-acts. A genuine act is creative or redemptive, and, as I have tried to show elsewhere, Christ is the hero of *Paradise Lost* by default, because he is the only character in it who performs a genuine act. In Shelley, Prometheus has many of the qualities of Milton's Satan, and because the heavenly god of Shelley's poem is evil Prometheus' Satanic defiance has our sympathy. But Shelley had noted in his Preface that Satan's defiance of God is chiefly what keeps God in business. When Prometheus withdraws his curse, therefore, he becomes an Adam instead of a Satan, or, in Blake's terms, he moves from the bound state of Luvah to the unbound state of Albion. Prometheus is not a poet: he hears and understands what the poets are saying, but he cannot himself hear what the poet hears. Being immortal, the world of death, sleep and dream is not a separate world for him, hence he cannot formulate a message that is conveyed only to mortals. In his bound state, he represents, not Man, but men, who discover that, in the words of *The Defence of Poetry,* "there is no portal of expression from the caverns of the spirit which they inhabit into the universe of things." Mortal men can respond individually but not as a group, because they are too frightened to love. Shelley is never tired of quoting Tasso's remark that only God and the poet are creators, but Prometheus is closer to the universal human mind of Shelley's essay *On Life,* of which Shelley says that it perceives but does not create. Mary Shelley's *Frankenstein* is a creator, in a sense, and this story, which is subtitled "The Modern Prometheus," suggests some of the difficulties that man would get into if he simply tried to replace his projected god with himself. That is, we now perceive the world as a mechanical order, in the degenerate form of habit or familiarity; if we try to create our own world in the same image, we shall produce a technological monstrosity.

It is not, therefore, a creative act by which Prometheus frees himself: it is rather that he establishes a situation in which the creative utterance can be finally heard in its full meaning. Prometheus desires to hear his original curse pronounced again: this would normally symbolize the beginning of a new cycle of repeated pain. He is man defiantly subjective, trapped by an objective Jupiter who has obtained his power from him. Yet he is prolonging his pain and Jupiter's power by his defiance, because he is continuing the subject-object separation, continuing to be an anguish confronting an absurdity. The withdrawing of the curse means either that he has lost hope, as Earth at first thinks, or that he has ceased to keep Jupiter in existence by making himself the other half of the Jupiter vision. The latter is true, and hence the mortal power of responding to the voice of poetry coincides with a newly courageous consciousness in which it becomes fully communicable.

The typical theme of successful heroic action is the quest, the deliverance of the king's daughter from the dragon by the virtuous and punctual stranger-knight. This myth is incorporated into Christianity, where Christ kills the dragon of death and delivers his Bride, the Church. Milton had already, in *Paradise Regained*, presented this theme in its paradoxical form: Christ's triumph consists essentially of an act of suffering and humiliation, and the deliverer is a victim who has to be swallowed by the dragon before he can trample it underfoot. In Shelley the quest appears in the still more paradoxical form of the *renounced* quest. Similarly in Wagner's *Ring*, the quest has to be given up and the stolen ring put back where it was before man can outgrow the gods and the palace of Wotan can go up in flames. The popular Anglicized rifacimento of Wagner, Tolkien's *Lord of the Rings*, does not have quite this theological dimension, but it uses the same renounced-quest theme. Like the definitive act of vision which is the goal of so many Eastern religions, what Prometheus does is not a doing but an arrest of what he has habitually been doing. The force of habit, which is what Prometheus' defiance has become, is a kind of inert or mechanical energy which slowly congeals the objective world into a predictable order by a predictable reaction to it. To stop the current of habit is like rolling back the waves of the Red Sea, and bringing a new world into being.

In *The Revolt of Islam,* where the St. George and Dragon conception of revolution is very prominent, the central figures are victims who triumph only in a spiritual world, like Christian martyrs. But Prometheus triumphs by refusing to continue as a victim of a tyrant who does not have to be there. The traditional myth said that man "fell" in the past, and inherits an evil he cannot now resist. Shelley's myth says that as man put his tyrant into power, man can annul that power, and the fall can be annihilated at any time by an act of vision. Thus the equivalent of faith in Shelley is a gnosis which is an act of vision and consciousness, and which is therefore not an act in Milton's sense, nor a pseudo-act, nor a parody-act, but a withdrawal from action. It might even be called an achievement of a state of nothingness or void in which reality appears. According to St. Augustine the fall began the experience of time as we now have it. Similarly the annulment of the fall creates a moment of time or *kairos,* the Car of the Hour, in which Jupiter, the son of Cronos (identified with Chronos or time in later myth), is dethroned by Eternity, the name Demogorgon gives to himself. What we ordinarily think of as action takes place in a time which annihilates everything. In the withdrawal from action which is also an expansion of consciousness, time is transformed into what is traditionally its unfallen form: the dance or expression of energy and exuberance in life:

> *Once the hungry Hours were hounds*
>   *Which chased the day like a bleeding deer,*
> *And it limped and stumbled with many wounds*
>   *Through the nightly dells of the desert year.*

> *But now, oh weave the mystic measure*
>   *Of music, and dance, and shapes of light,*
> *Let the Hours, and the spirits of might and pleasure,*
>   *Like the clouds and sunbeams, unite.*

If I seem to exaggerate the importance of Prometheus' recall of his curse, it is to emphasize the unity of theme in the poem. It is almost literally true to say that nothing happens in *Prometheus Unbound*. Man achieves a state of awareness in which he is no longer trying to revenge himself on a tyrant he has created, and so is no longer divided against himself. Up till then, messages of love and hope have been coming through poetry and dreams, and nature, to quote the very un-Shelleyan St. Paul, has been groaning and travailing in pain. But now the central authentic voice of the imagination can be heard: Asia is led to the profoundest depth of the oracular world by Panthea's dream which she had forgotten, and Jupiter vanishes into the phantasm that he always really was. *Prometheus Unbound* is Shelley's definitive poem not only because it incorporates Shelley's central and distinctive myth, but because it has attained the plotless or actionless narrative which seems to be characteristic of the mythopoeic genre. Of Shelley's first two essays in a definitive poem, *Queen Mab* is carried along by its argument: it is in the eighteenth-century tradition of the didactic poem. In *The Revolt of Islam* there is a plot of sorts, and a great nuisance it is: we notice that whenever the imagery goes fuzzy the reason usually is that the plot has given another spasmodic lurch. Shelley could construct plot well enough when it was appropriate to the genre he was using, as it is in *The Cenci*. But the unity of *Prometheus Unbound* is the unity of a theme which exists all at once in various aspects, and where the narrative can therefore only move from the periphery into the center and out again.

We notice, in the spatial imagery of the poem, that the central point, the cave of Demogorgon, is, consistently with the general outlines of the Romantic cosmos, in depths far below ordinary experience. Except for one remarkable image of an avalanche, all the revolutionary energy in the poem rises from caves, volcanoes, the floors of lakes, and seas: even Jupiter expects a renewal of his power to come from below, and speaks of "the Incarnation, which ascends." There are many passages in the poem suggesting that, like many other poets, Shelley associates the ideas of fall and deluge, and that man is now symbolically under water. The struggle between Prometheus and Jupiter is thus in part a struggle for the control of the ocean, represented on the one side by Prometheus' love for Asia, a daughter of the Oceanides, and on the other by Jupiter's marriage to Thetis the Nereid. When Prometheus is freed, Atlantis immediately reappears from the depths of the ocean. Similarly in Blake, Atlantis is the genuine or spiritual form of England's green and pleasant land, which is restored as soon as man has drained the "Sea of Time and Space" off the top of his mind.

We have seen that the Kantian riddle of a distinction between things as known and things in themselves informs a great deal of Romantic imagery. In literature the noumenal world becomes a mysterious world hidden within or behind the world of ordinary experience—for while philosophers may be able to escape from such spatial and diagrammatic metaphors as "within" or "behind," poets never make any pretense of being able to do so. For many Romantics, especially the more conservative ones, a world which by definition cannot be known by ordinary experience becomes sinister as soon as it is translated from the language of concept into the language of concern. At best it encourages a greater reliance on forms of consciousness which seem to evade or by-pass ordinary experience. Shelley's view of this situation is less skeptical and more Platonic. There is a world "behind" the objects we see, and a world "behind" the subjects that perceive it: these hidden worlds are the same world; poetry is the voice of that world; and the vision of love, which contains and transforms all opposites, can realize it. We are closer here to the other great Romantic construct formulated by Hegel. For Shelley a universal idea is actualizing itself in the world by the containing and transforming of opposites: this idea is the idea of liberty, and liberty is a creative force in a cosmological sense, the principle of order in the chaos, or debased creation, of Jupiter's tyranny and Prometheus' torment. Apostrophizing liberty, Shelley says:

> *But this divinest universe*
> *Was yet a chaos and a curse,*
> *For thou wert not.*

For liberty is the actualization of the new world that the arrest of Prometheus' habitual revenge-energy has brought into being.

The liberating of Prometheus is, up to a point, something like a Hegelian liberation, an expanding of consciousness which destroys the antithesis of subject and object and creates a larger identity, as the "mask" falls from man and the "veil" from nature. The transcending of opposites in Shelley is expressed by the myth of the mar-

riage with a sister-bride. The release of Prometheus also releases the Eros-figure of the Spirit of the Earth, who differs
from Ariel in being a partaker of human and sexual love.
His sister-bride is the snow-maiden of the moon, now ready
to be thawed out and brought to life like Hermione or Pyg-
malion's statue. Similarly in *Epipsychidion* the antithesis of
Death and Life is also described as "twin babes, a sister
and a brother." The symbol of the sister-bride has a scan-
dalous and incestuous sound to unemancipated ears, but
what it represents is the unifying power of Eros. In the
state of the bound Prometheus, fear is primary, and we
love only what we fear the least. Genuine love does not,
like the soul in Emily Dickinson, select its own society and
shut the door: wherever it exists it creates liberty, equality,
and, along with fraternity, sorority. "Incest," says Shelley
demurely, "is, like many other incorrect things, a very po-
etical circumstance."

For the state of the bound Prometheus the obvious complementary symbol is that of the coy, teasing, elusive *femme
fatale,* representing an objective world that man never
really possesses. Shelley understands this symbol, but he
has a strong moral dislike of it. Twice it appears offstage.
It is the source of Alastor's nympholepsy, and in *Julian
and Maddalo* a discussion about what it is that prevents
man from becoming free focuses on a symbol of a madman
whose madness and imprisonment have resulted from a
sinister female influence. The Medusa image also appears
in some of the shorter lyrics. But in general the female in
Shelley is an "epipsyche," or what Blake would call an
emanation, the beauty that embodies the vision of love, the
"Asia" or "married land" of the Biblical Beulah. In Shelley, as in Blake, the mother, especially the Mother Earth
of *Prometheus Unbound,* usually represents a state of im-
perfection which has yet to be transcended.

Naturally, the antithesis of earth and heaven is also transcended in the liberation of Prometheus. The three main stages in passing through this antithesis are recorded in the *Ode to Heaven,* a poem closely related to *Prometheus Unbound.* Here a first spirit speaks of Heaven as an abode

> *Of that power which is the glass*
> *Wherein man his nature sees.*

A second spirit sees this abode as an underground cave, a chrysalis to be burst through by an awakening mind, and a third spirit sees it as a transformation of what we now live in on earth. Similarly, Panthea remarks that a vision she sees is "not earthly," but it proves to be the vision of the Spirit of the Earth, the Eros-figure released along with Prometheus. In the mystical marriage of man and nature, the green world returns; the music of the spheres is heard again; human society is suddenly full of love and equality.

In the older schema a return to the unfallen world would carry with it a complete regeneration of the natural order: everything from bad weather to thorns on the rose came with the fall, and would disappear at its end. In Shelley's symbolism too we gather that the deadly nightshade is no longer poisonous and that the tyrants of the animal kingdom, such as behemoth and leviathan, are disappearing along with human tyrants. Here Shelley is following traditional symbolic models, such as Virgil's Fourth Eclogue and the Bible, where behemoth and leviathan are explicitly linked with Egypt and Babylon.

Yet a miraculous transformation of the order of nature is clearly not as consistent with Shelley's poetic postulates as it would be with Dante's, for example, where an omnipotent will could be invoked to bring about the transformation. Much in Shelley's account of the released exuberance and inner happiness of subhuman nature, and of man's freedom in it, depends, like the corresponding themes in Wordsworth, on a distanced and aesthetic view of nature, a north-temperate-zone view, as it has been called, of a nature largely tamed by human settlement. What is being described is the attaining of an identity with the inner process of nature and a transcendence of the old subject-object separation. But the terms of the description ignore most of what seems to us the real inner process of nature, the cruelty and ruthless fight to survive which impress us so deeply in this post-Darwinian age, and revert to a new kind of contemplative objectivity. One often finds in Shelley, perhaps most explicitly in *Mont Blanc,* a sense that the theme of the renewal of man and nature by a union between them, which poetry attempts to communicate through emotions of serenity, sublimity, and the like, does not fit into the conceptual language of the same and the other. It is no good rejecting a tyrannical Jupiter merely to fall into a childish belief that God has really designed nature for our convenience.

The question involved here, which meets us again in Keats, is central to the whole Romantic movement, and needs to be formulated with some care. Of course Shelley's main theme is the emancipation of man, to which the spirits of nature form a chorus. The suggestion is that a great deal of what we see in nature reflects our own condition: we see cruelty and oppression because that is our own state, and if we could escape from this state we might see many of the same things as exuberance and joy. A liberated vision would show us that things shine by their own light, not by the reflection of ours. The suffering in nature is identical with the suffering of man; and similarly, the creative power of man is identical with the beauty and splendor of nature.

We have spoken of the importance of occult imagery in Romanticism as symbolizing the new kind of natural knowledge that man is developing, and to this imagery Shelley's nature-spirits and the like belong. When Hamlet says to Horatio, apropos of his father's ghost, that there are more things in heaven and earth than are dreamt of in your philosophy, he is thinking of "philosophy" as the knowledge of a visible objective world which may be extended or contradicted by the knowledge of an invisible but equally objective one. Occult imagery in Beddoes or Shelley, on the other hand, represents rather the boundary line between perceived and created worlds. Ghosts and such are usually interpreted in terms of the subject-object split: either they are there and objective, or not there and subjective. But in Romantic imagery they represent the kind of vision that a highly developed imagination might attain of a world of awakened human powers. This is the world of Zoroaster meeting himself in the garden, things which are partly subjective shadows "in here" and partly objective shadows "out there" becoming their unified substances.

It appears therefore that in Shelley, as in Beddoes (on whom of course Shelley was a major influence), this world of realized unity with nature is also the world which we enter or can enter at death. If life is the dream of the Earth-Spirit, then, perhaps, death is the shadow of that dream rejoining its substance. The life we live, a one-dimensional progress toward death, is half of reality: the other half is the contrary movement that comes through dreams, inspiration, and poetry. Zoroaster meeting his own image thus is or symbolizes the totality that we experience as an antithesis of life *and* death:

> *Death is the veil that those who live call life:*
> *They sleep, and it is lifted.*

At the end of *The Revolt of Islam*, the hero and heroine, who are apparently being burned alive at the stake as sacrifices to superstition, are really sailing down a river in a boat toward Paradise. T. S. Eliot later developed a similar imagery of the shadow of life rejoining its substance at death out of Christian sources, more particularly Dante. *Marina* and *Ash Wednesday* are much indebted to the passage in the *Purgatorio* where Dante, entering Eden, becomes as he would have been had man not fallen. Yet Eliot recognized his similarity to Shelley also on this point, and quotes the Zoroaster passage in *The Cocktail Party* in connection with the martyrdom of Celia.

As soon as Prometheus' deliverance is under way, Asia, like the lovers in *The Revolt of Islam*, finds herself on an enchanted boat traveling in the reverse direction from ordinary experience, like the poet's upstream movement at the end of Yeats' *Tower,* or Eliot's Phlebas who "passed the stages of his age and youth" while being drowned:

> *We have passed Age's icy caves,*
> *And Manhood's dark and tossing waves,*
> *And Youth's smooth ocean, smiling to betray:*
> *Beyond the glassy gulfs we flee*
> *Of shadow-peopled Infancy,*
> *Through Death and Birth, to a diviner day.*

The real world of death being that of ordinary life proceeding toward death, the world which is mysterious and hidden from us is the world of immortality. In his earlier essay *On a Future State,* and elsewhere, Shelley rejects the conception of the survival of the individual ego after physical death. But he retains his own view of immortality, a view which is more closely related to the *Phaedo* than to the New Testament. His immortality is not that of individual lives, but of such human states as love and joy and desire and the perception of beauty, which are eternally a part of man's identity with the Earth-Spirit, or whatever God is. From these states human life is projected, and back to them life is withdrawn. These immortal states or moods of humanity were formerly called gods, and were perverted into different kinds of tyranny. Properly understood, it is only the states connected with hope and love and knowledge that are immortal: Venus is immortal, but Jupiter and Mars are not. To reverse the aphorism of Browning, there must be heaven; meanwhile there is hell. In *The Sensitive Plant* Shelley describes a paradisal garden under the care of a lady like Dante's Matilda: both lady and garden die in the cycle of nature, but the conclusion is:

> *For love, and beauty, and delight,*
> *There is no death nor change: their might*
> *Exceeds our organs, which endure*
> *No light, being themselves obscure.*

The fact that Shelley is a revolutionary thinker does not necessarily make him a spokesman of political revolution of either the popular or the nationalistic type. He shows sympathy with both, but in the vision of the bound Prometheus the French Revolution, like the coming of Christ, is an effort at freedom which failed. It was an attempt to dethrone Jupiter by a force that merely continued his tyranny, because it did not alter the mental attitude that kept Jupiter in existence. Similarly in Beddoes, the genuine nemesis of the Duke does not proceed from Isbrand's seizure of his ducal power, which merely subjects Isbrand to the same kind of nemesis. What liberates Prometheus is a state of consciousness, an act of vision, which enables the creative power of man to emerge. Political rebellions may be the effects of such an act, but they cannot cause it. Shelley's sympathy with the national or self-determining revolutions that followed the French Revolution has much to do with being closer to them in time, feeling that he can take their results for granted ("The Spanish Peninsula is already free," as he says in the Preface to *Hellas*). *The Revolt of Islam,* whose theme is professedly political, has very little in it that one can directly attach to contemporary or even predicted political events, and even the politically inflammatory poems, such as *Song to the Men of England,* are not attached to a suggested program of action. He does have an early manifesto of human rights, but it would not be easy to base a political or revolutionary party on it. All this is extremely obvious, but it is not always realized that a deficiency in a nonpoetical area may be, not merely irrelevant to a poet, but a positive source of strength in his poetry.

When Mary Shelley remarks that "Shelley believed that mankind had only to will that there should be no evil, and there would be none," the word "only" reflects the perplexity of most people confronted with apocalyptic thinking —and perhaps too the perplexity even of those engaged in it. The effort of will she speaks of, which is, like the corresponding will in Christianity, more of a renunciation of will than an exercise of it, is the supreme effort to which all mankind's history has been leading up. After it has been made, perhaps, we can say "was this all we had to do?" but before it occurs we should not underestimate its difficulty. Yet *Prometheus Unbound,* even so, leaves us with the feeling of something left out. The emancipation of man it portrays is purely spatial, and, so to speak, scientific. As man's mind expands into the secrets of nature in a mental consummation, we simply pass from the night of the present into the light of the future. As the spirits say in the hideous but cheerful doggerel in which most of the fourth act is written:

> *We come from the mind*
> *Of human kind*
> *Which was late so dusk, and obscene, and blind,*
> *Now 'tis an ocean*
> *Of clear emotion,*
> *A heaven of serene and mighty motion.*

But there is no temporal dimension; the dead past simply buries its dead; the oracles of tyranny fall silent like the similar oracles in Milton's *Nativity Ode,* and what time has annihilated remains annihilated. It is true that the motive force of Prometheus' liberation is the car of the "Spirit of the Hour," but it is not clearly explained how it gets to be the right hour, at least in the context of history. Like Dante, we scramble out into the light of day on the other side of the earth, leaving the hell of history behind us like a bad dream. History is a nightmare from which we awake, as the very Shelleyan Stephen Dedalus remarked. Yet the feeling that any genuine liberation would also be a harrowing of hell, a liberation of the past and of history, clearly haunted Shelley: it is central to *Hellas* and to the troubled and unfinished *Triumph of Life.* It is also central to the argument of *The Defence of Poetry.*

Though never explicitly stated, one of the central ideas in *The Defence of Poetry* is that of an authentic response to poetry, reading it not merely as a product of its age, but as the prophetic voice of human imagination itself. Every great work of literature speaks with this prophetic voice under the disguise of the limitations and anxieties of its own time. Thus it is imagination mixed up with, and concealed by, a more conceptual type of thinking. The contemporary age, according to the essay of Peacock which provoked Shelley's "defence," is a "brazen age" in which the poet is a vestigial survival of an antiquated way of thinking. To Shelley, on the contrary, it is an age when modern thinking can finally become completely separated from poetic thinking. A good deal of modern thought, as represented by the "Paley and Malthus" referred to in the Preface to *Prometheus Unbound,* is aggressive: it attacks and defends and refutes, and its chief motivation is ultimately to rationalize arbitrary power in whatever form.

There are of course liberal conceptual thinkers, Locke, Gibbon, Voltaire, Rousseau, and others listed in the *Defence.* But even they are of limited social value compared to the great poets and to the more visionary philosophers, because they preserve the aggressive and argumentative form of thinking that can hardly, by definition, present anything except half-truths. In the *Essay on Christianity* Rousseau's doctrine of equality is compared with the genuine teachings of Jesus, before their perversion by Christianity, and the comparison of course is intended to be high praise for Jesus. But in *The Triumph of Life* Rousseau appears to have become the typical bastard poet, whose influence promoted political instead of imaginative revolution, and who consequently merely helped to prolong the tyranny of time. Aggressive thinking makes a great parade of "stubborn facts" and "hard and fast" distinctions, and other synonyms, to use a post-Shelleyan image, of the domineering male in erection. Poetic thinking, being mythical, does not distinguish or create antitheses: it goes on and on, linking analogy to analogy, identity to identity, and containing, without trying to refute, all opposition and objection. This means, not that it is merely facile or liquid thinking without form, but that it is the dialectic of love: it treats whatever it encounters as another form of itself. By the same token it is never abstract: abstraction is the product of a repetition of experience without fresh thought.

There is an implicit historical dialectic in the argument of *The Defence of Poetry*. A primitive language, Shelley says, "is in itself the chaos of a cyclic poem," and as history goes on, more and more is unrolled of "that great poem, which all poets, like the co-operating thoughts of one great mind, have built up since the beginning of the world." And as poetry thus develops, we begin to understand how to read it as a product of man's eternal imagination, and not of his temporary fears and superstitions. In time, poetry continues to "reanimate . . . the sleeping, the cold, the buried image of the past." Hence a renewing of human life coincides with the attaining of the power of hearing what it is that poetry is really saying. We thus arrive at conceptions corresponding to the Christian doctrine of the invasion of time, at a certain point in time, by eternity, though the point of this invasion is in the near future. When Shelley speaks of "the mediator and the redeemer, Time," it is clear that he is thinking of liberty as a force that grows in time and redeems history, and is not simply a force leaping out of time like a fish out of water.

There is nothing in this sense of the deliverance of history which is at all inconsistent with what we find in *Prometheus Unbound*. But in *Hellas* Shelley says, rather more clearly, that the future is the past come to life, and that when this resurrection is accomplished, past and future both disappear into an eternal present, when the tyranny of time—that is, the clock time that never ceases to be time —shall be no more. Such a conception deepens and enlarges the vision of *Prometheus Unbound* with another principle, expressed by Eliot as "Only through time is time conquered." As already suggested, this historical vision is closer to that of traditional Christianity. In the Prologue to *Hellas* Satan is reproached by Christ (true, still a Hellenized Christ whose love is an *eros*) for having only a cyclical view of history, in which the future can never escape from the past. The repetition prophesied by the final chorus is not a vision of the same thing happening again, but of the old renewed. When Ahasuerus says:

> *The Past*
> *Now stands before thee like an Incarnation*
> *Of the To-come*

he is celebrating a theme of, so to speak, discarnation, in which the Jewish hope for a coming Messiah and the Christian hope of a second coming are at one.

The principle of authentic reading is particularly important in connection with the two chief poetic influences on Shelley. These were Plato and Dante, both of whom have been accused of laying up their treasures in a remote heaven too free of moth and rust to be of much concern to human life, of burying their talents in the sky. But for Shelley Plato was not a philosopher of dualism or objective idealism, creating imaginary states of tyranny and fanaticism, nor was Dante a visionary of a future and unending triumph of Jupiter. Both were for Shelley poets of Eros, celebrating a love that turned human society into a festive symposium and raised woman to a *vita nuova* of equal dignity with man. Shelley puts Eros into the peculiarly modern position of a revolutionary and explosive force. In this position his Eros anticipates the Eros of Freud, but Shelley has nothing of Freud's despondent resignation to the tyranny of anxiety. For Shelley Eros will destroy the world if too long repressed, and recreate it if released, and hence Shelley has envisioned, more clearly than any other poet, the apocalyptic dilemma of modern man.

Endymion:

The Romantic Epiphanic

We have been dealing with various aspects of a central theme of the Romantic movement: a distinction between two kinds of reality. There is the reality out there, which is studied by science and the reason from the point of view of a conscious subject perceiving objects. There is also the reality that we bring into being through an act of creation, which is the special function of the arts, and which Romanticism regards as a larger structure of reality including the given reality of experience. The arts illustrate the form of the world that man is trying to create out of the world he is in. They do many other things as well, but there is a powerful moral force working in them either to express an ideal, illustrating such a world positively, or to become ironic, illustrating it negatively by contrast. The ideal aspect of poetry seemed more obvious to the Romantics, just as the ironic aspect seems more obvious to us. Everybody needs a sense of reality about the world out there, but, for the Romantics, everybody also needs some kind of vision of a better world that man can create. We can use this vision as a standard by which we can judge the "real" world according to our ideals; as a model to work from when acting according to an ideal vision; and as a means of recognizing a better order of things when it is presented to us, whether in the arts or in life.

The Romantic myth is the form in which the Romantic poet expresses the recovery, for man, of what he formerly ascribed to gods, heroes, or the forces of nature. When man is recognized to be a myth-making animal, mythical language is also recognized to be the language, not for what is true, but for what could be made true. Mythology, thus, with Romanticism, as we have seen, ceases to be fables about the actions of superior powers and becomes a structure of human concern. It thereby takes over some aspects of religion. This does not mean that poetry becomes a religion or a substitute for religion. It means that what was formerly a structure of belief understood rationally, through doctrinal and conceptual statement, is now, from the Romantic movement onward, increasingly understood and interpreted imaginatively, as a structure of what might and could be true. Naturally, this change from what we have called a "closed" to an "open" social use of mythology is bound to make changes in the structure of comprehension itself, chiefly in the direction of making it more flexible. In his speculations about the world as a "vale of soulmaking," Keats makes it clear that he thinks of his poetry as going in the direction of becoming the interpreter of a religion more tolerant and more genuinely catholic than any institutional form of religion.

Traditionally, man is born with a myth of a golden world or lost paradise built into him, through his descent from Adam. From the Romantic point of view, this is an alienation myth expressing man's sense that his consciousness has made him lose his identity with nature. Man should learn to think of this pastoral myth as a vision of innocence, not an innocence forever lost under a curse, but an innocence which is present in the mind and is a potentially creative power. Such innocence can, when guided by the poetic imagination, be realized in experience, and can thereby assimilate experience to its own form. When man is born, the sense of identity with nature remains unborn, and the quest of the soul is to bring it to birth.

The opening lines of *Endymion* explain to us how this Edenic myth exists in our own minds, in the form of an awareness of beauty. Such an awareness is not a mere solace in sorrow, though it is also that, but a more intensely experienced kind of reality. The elements of ordinary experience, our realization of the world out there, are consciousness and sensation, and these, at a pitch of greater mental intensity, become joy and the perception of the beautiful. In ordinary experience truth is what we see and understand: in more intense experience, where truth is created as well as recognized, truth is beauty. Whoever is saying this in the *Ode on a Grecian Urn*, Keats is certainly saying it in *Endymion*. The poem is devoted to the theme of realizing beauty, making it true by creating it. Keats, like Shelley, thinks in triads, and in a letter he divides reality into three aspects: real things, "semireal" things "which require a greeting of the Spirit to make them wholly exist," and "Nothings" which are "dignified by an ardent pursuit." Without the third element, nothing made something by effort, the distinctively creative aspect of experience would not be there: without the other two, creation would be a private and subjective fantasy identical with the dream.

Keats was, of course, deeply interested in the relation between sleep and poetry, the dreaming and the creative operations of the mind. This is partly the reason for his attraction to Endymion as a hero, for in the myths Endymion spends most of his time asleep. A remarkable passage in the fourth book of *Endymion* connects the wish-fulfillment element in dreams with the ambition of the poet which drives him to realize his aims. What is real about the dream is its illusion, its absence of objectivity, and the poet, like the dreamer, strives to *contain* his world. But ultimately "The poet and the dreamer are distinct." The imagination, Keats says, is like the dream of Adam, who awoke to find his dream true. Art, as Plato says, is a dream for awakened minds, and the poet's function is to make the vision of beauty the awakened and conscious opposite of a dream.

The student of *Endymion* finds it a difficulty that Keats was so rigorous a critic of his own work, and felt so quickly that he had outgrown *Endymion*. If he had felt more like defending it, instead of going on to even greater things, we should at least have had more hints from him about what he was trying to do in it. As it is, there are only three of much significance. *Endymion* is, Keats says, a "huge attempt," as it obviously is, and its entire action consists of "one bare circumstance," presumably the process of realizing the dream of Diana with which the poem begins. He also says that he himself learned far more by plunging into the poem than he would have done by more cautious procedures.

Picking up this last remark, we see that *Endymion* represents, among other things, Keats' absorption of the traditional structure of symbolism which he had learned chiefly from Spenser and Milton. This structure, we remember, is most easily understood, for literary purposes, as a schema of four "levels" of imagery: heaven, the innocent world, the ordinary world, and hell. In *Paradise Lost* the top level is heaven, the place of the presence of God; then comes the Garden of Eden, or the unfallen world generally; then the world of history and ordinary experience, described only by anticipation; and at the bottom are the kingdoms of Satan and Chaos. In *The Faerie Queene* there is a heaven above, referred to in a very few passages, notably the last stanza of the Mutabilitie Cantoes; then a world of "Faerie," where the main action of the poem takes place; then the world of history and ordinary experience, described obliquely through allegory; and then a demonic world from which monsters and other sinister creatures emerge. In Dante's *Commedia*—a later influence on Keats—there is heaven, symbolized by the planetary spheres; then the Garden of Eden, along with the purgatorial upward movement toward it; then the Italy of 1300, described by allusion though not the scene of any of the action; and then hell. In all three poets, we notice, the third level, the world of ordinary experience, remains offstage, introduced through some special device like allegory or allusion. In all three, again, the second level is a pastoral world, a vision of innocence and spontaneity where the inhabitants are instinctively poets, and where the conditions of human life are simplified to the essentials. In Dante this applies primarily to the glimpse of Eden at the end of the *Purgatorio* rather than to the purgatorial process itself which leads up to it, but in attaining to Eden Dante recovers his own childhood innocence, not in his individual life but in his inheritance as a son of Adam.

In Spenser, who is the closest of the three to *Endymion*, there are two features of particular interest. First, the third or ordinary world, besides being referred to in allegory, also appears symbolically as a *sexual* world, presided over by Venus, and represented by the satyrs, whose sexual energy is natural but not quite innocent, halfway between human love and demonic lust. Second, the world of "Faerie" is a mythical world, not a different place from the ordinary world, but the same world in which the moral and imaginative realization of a higher kind of experience takes place. Similarly, Dante's Eden is on top of the mountain of purgatory, which is on the surface of the same world that we live in. Spenser's interest in the realization of the greater powers in the soul is, for most of the poem, moral rather than imaginative in its expression and imagery. In other words, Faerie in Spenser is mostly a purgatorial world, like the corresponding world in Dante. But Spenser does have one great vision in which it is the imaginative rather than the moral powers that are realized. The first book of the poem as we have it outlines the central Biblical myth of redemption, in the traditional terms of a movement from God to man through grace and the Word; the last or sixth book seems to be focused on the human counterpart of this, the legend of courtesy, where grace and healing words appear in their human context. The poet himself, symbolized as Colin Clout, plays a part in the climactic scene in this legend on Mount Acidale. Keats' special fondness for the sixth book, the story of Calidore, is obvious enough.

The action of *Endymion* begins in the second of four worlds, the world corresponding to Spenser's Faerie and to Dante's and Milton's Eden, where Adam had his dream. In the earlier poets this is the world man lost long ago, and can regain only through a long process of discipline. In Keats, who is adapting the traditional structure to a Romantic outlook, it is the world of the pastoral myth in which poetic creation begins, a world still present and potential. It is the state that we work from, not the place we return to: in his letters Keats calls it the "chamber of maiden thought." The word "maiden" indicates a youthful and pre-sexual aspect of life, which the prominence given to Endymion's sister emphasizes. The phrase also indicates the reason for a curious feature of the poem, a feature that has put off many readers, including, to judge from his revised preface, Keats himself. We first meet the poet-hero in a state of deep melancholy, and recognize the old Courtly Love convention. This is the same state of helpless pining grief in which we first meet Romeo; fair enough. But why should a poet as vigorous as Keats, who so disliked the thought of being made "a pet lamb in a sentimental farce," have created a hero so languid that his sister has to move the branches out of his way as he walks through the woods?

The reason is that Endymion's world is the imprisoning, paralyzing world of dream, the dream being partly about a great achievement in the future, and so accompanied by all the anxieties that go with the dislocation of time. We have said that when man is born, his vision of innocence remains unborn, and has to be brought to birth. Endymion is not literally unborn, but his achievement is, and his world has the fragility that goes with something that is only potentially alive. We may compare *The Book of Thel*, by the equally vigorous Blake, with its shadowy dissolving imagery, where things melt into other things without taking on definite existence, a world Thel could have escaped from by getting born, which she fails to do. Similarly, the first book of *Endymion* introduces us to a world in which spirits "melt away and thaw," as though the mind and its moods had no permanent reality:

> *Apollo's upward fire*
> *Made every eastern cloud a silvery pyre*
> *Of brightness so unsullied, that therein*
> *A melancholy spirit well might win*
> *Oblivion, and melt out his essence fine*
> *Into the winds.*

We may also recall the sensitive heroines of Gothic novels, already referred to. In reading romance, we often have the feeling that we are in a magical world held together by the spell of chastity or purity, which sexual experience would instantly destroy. Wonderland depends on an unawakened Alice. Usually this chastity is associated with the heroine, and the typical romance ends when the heroine approaches her first sexual communion. In our day we are so aware of the absurdity of this notion of "purity" in actual life that we overlook its significance as a literary convention. The vision of purity to us suggests rather an onanistic fantasy involving physical but not sexual contact. Byron expressed himself with his customary forthrightness on this subject in connection with Keats, and it was doubtless a suspicion of the same quality in Shelley that led Mark Rampion, in Aldous Huxley's *Point Counterpoint,* to call Shelley a white slug. Rampion is a mask for D. H. Lawrence, and Lawrence had acute anxieties on such matters. In our day we can afford to be more tolerant, besides recognizing that Shelley and Keats use their conventions of purity for the express purpose of shattering them.

In some versions of the four "levels" the second one is an innocent vision attainable in ordinary life, in childhood, in wish, in dream, or in romance. In this context the vision is usually temporary or illusory. This is particularly true if it remains a private and unshared vision, like sentimentalized childhood memories and other nostalgic pastoral themes. In Eliot's *Burnt Norton* the brief glimpse of the rose-garden is a vision of this sort. Here the intruder into the garden is driven out because "human kind cannot bear very much reality." Endymion has been brought up in the garden world, and his sense of reality is reversed, but the impulse to get away from it is present in him too. We notice a feeling of *guilt* in Endymion, of a responsibility not yet assumed, which pushes him out of his world into a lower one. This feeling of guilt recurs in Thel, in Rasselas in his Abyssinian prison-paradise, and in a later and very different treatment of the same myth, the chapter on the world of the unborn in Butler's *Erewhon*. In Blake the state of innocence is a childhood state inevitably followed by experience; in Milton the foreknowledge of Adam's sin, which the reader certainly has whether God has it or not, also conveys a sense of the inevitable destruction of Eden. Even in Dante the sacramental machinery pulls the soul out of Eden into another paradise of stars, while the seeds of other forms of life fall back into our world.

Keats' pastoral world is a green world of forests and grassy clearings, innocent but still a part of the cycle of life and death, like Spenser's Faerie. In Spenser, Venus presides over this world as well as ours. Diana, by reason of her associations with virginity, the moon, and Queen Elizabeth, has in Spenser a somewhat specialized role: she appears in the Mutabilitie Cantoes as the goddess of the moon, the boundary of an eternal starry kingdom separated from our world of mutability, and the symbol of the ultimate vision of heaven or "Sabaoth's sight." Endymion, however, is traditionally the lover of Diana in her aspect as Phoebe the moon-goddess, and hence in Keats Endymion's quest is for the topmost world, or what corresponds to heaven. From this world he is completely separated, to his despair, when the poem opens. Endymion's society worships Pan, but Pan, though a fertility god, is also, by virtue of his name, a "symbol of immensity," the

> *Dread opener of the mysterious doors*
> *Leading to universal knowledge*

who is associated with Christ in Spenser's *Shepheards Calender*. The heaven of *Endymion* is therefore the place of the presence of Pan, an "Elysium" and "eternal spring" of final reunion and happiness. The old men of Endymion's society are on the verge of entering it, and it is also described in New Testament language as a world where lost lambs are found again. It is ordinarily reached by contemplation, to which Endymion proposes to devote himself at the end of the first book, but Endymion's real wish, and his destiny, is to enter it through his love for Diana (i.e., Phoebe) as the moon. He cannot approach Diana directly: the best known story about the disasters of doing so is the story of Actaeon, who is associated with the poet by Shelley in *Adonais*. Nor does Endymion realize, at this stage, that it is Diana whom he loves.

At the beginning of the *Inferno* Dante encounters three dangerous beasts: instead of facing them head-on he turns away and goes in the opposite direction, a direction which takes him through hell, purgatory, and paradise. On a small scale something parallel happens to Endymion: he is unable to go directly into the world of Pan and Phoebe above him, and has to go in the opposite direction, through the third and fourth levels of his poetic cosmos. These levels are associated respectively with earth and with water: the "visions of the earth" take up the second book and the adventures under the sea the third. We should expect, by analogy with the earlier epic poets, to find the earth-world associated with a loss of innocence and the development of experience, more particularly sexual experience, and to find the submarine world sinister and demonic. We do find this, but there are great and essential gains in the descent: all levels are morally ambivalent, with both apocalyptic and demonic aspects. Endymion is really acquiring, through the descent, something of the "universal knowledge" of the Pan world above him. He has to go down in search of truth before he can go up in search of beauty and discover that they are in fact the same point.

He has said of his own world that he can feel no roots in it:

> *Where soil is men grow,*
> *Whether to weeds or flowers; but for me,*
> *There is no depth to strike in.*

The purpose of his quest is to strike these roots into experience. Besides, these lower worlds are also worlds of Diana, in her full extent as the great *diva triformis* who is the moon in heaven, the virgin huntress of the forests of earth, and the queen of the underworld. Rilke compares the poet to an angel who contains all time and space, but is blind and looks into himself, the circumference of a total imaginative vision. Keats, speaking of the blind Homer, also thinks of the poet as encompassing the entire world of the *diva triformis* from the moon-drawn sea to the moon:

> *There is a triple sight in blindness keen;*
> *Such seeing hadst thou, as it once befel*
> *To Dian, Queen of Earth, and Heaven, and Hell.*

We have just referred to the rose-garden episode in *Burnt Norton*, and in a passage that curiously parallels it, Endymion finds a magic rose that bursts suddenly into bloom. A butterfly on the rose leads him, like Eliot's thrush, to a fountain, where the butterfly, whose name is presumably Psyche, turns into a nymph, and tells him that he must descend lower, down through the worlds of earth and water, to accomplish his quest. Both lower worlds are described as labyrinthine:

> *winding passages, where sameness breeds*
> *Vexing conceptions of some sudden change*

and the physical ups and downs of the landscape correspond roughly, though by no means invariably, to the symbolic ups and downs of the four levels. The two middle worlds of the cosmos are associated mainly with the color green, the heavenly and submarine extremities with blue. The middle two both belong to the cycle of nature, the images of Endymion's pastoral home being more particularly related to the earlier phases of the cycle, youth, spring, and dawn. It is sexual love that makes the cycle of nature go round, and the central image of this driving force in Spenser (though in Spenser it is located in the world of Faerie above) is the place of seed, or Garden of Adonis, where Adonis sleeps and dreams through the winter and revives to life in summer. Endymion's coming at the turn of the season helps to revive Adonis (unless his arrival at that time was coincidence, which seems unlikely), and several other figures of the same type of seasonal and dying-god mythology are introduced, including a reference to Vertumnus and Pomona and a beautiful if somewhat inconclusive vision of Cybele. In *A Midsummer Night's Dream* there is a reference to "A fair vestal throned by the west," with the customary overtones of Queen Elizabeth, Diana, and the moon. Cupid shoots an arrow at her, which falls

short of her: its trajectory, symbolizing the cycle of life and
death under the moon, falls on a flower and turns it
purple, the red or purple flower being the emblem of the
Eros-Thanatos world of the gods of sexual love and death.
This symbol appears in the bed of "ditamy, and poppies
red" in the prelude to Endymion's vision, and a "cloudy
Cupid" with his arrows is also introduced toward the end
of the first book. The rhythm of vegetable life reviving from
death is picked up in the image of green plants bursting
through what appears to be the floor of a temple in the
second book.

The visions of the earth, then, have two aspects: one a
stage in the developing and maturing of Endymion's mind,
the other a stage in the discovery of the conditions of a
lower and more sinister world than the one he was brought
up in. The positive stage is represented by Endymion's own
sexual experience with the Indian maid, the story of Alpheus and Arethusa forming a chorus to it. The initiation
into the world of Eros is both a fall (loss of innocence) and
an advance to a greater maturity. Arethusa is a nymph of
Diana, who on this level is the elusive virgin huntress, occasionally glimpsed but never possessed, and Arethusa's
complaints tell us how sexual union brings about a desire
for a still more complete union which it cannot satisfy,
hence it is as much a frustration and an upsetting of balance as it is a satisfaction. And yet the reality of the experience as an incarnation of love is unanswerable: Endymion's possession of the Indian maid is for him what birth
would have been for Blake's Thel, a new life which, although it is also a form of death, as every new life is, also
gives him the roots in experience that he lacked before:

> *Now I have tasted her sweet soul to the core*
> *All other depths are shallow: essences,*

Once spiritual, are like muddy lees,
Meant but to fertilize my earthly root.

The other aspect of this journey through the earth, the discovery of a lower phase of being, follows the normal Romantic pattern. We said that the Romantic myth sees man as fallen from an identity *with* nature into a state of individual and subjective consciousness, identity *as* himself. When Endymion descends into the earth he also descends into this more subjective state, cutting off the more intimate contact with his natural environment that he possessed earlier. Such phrases as "The journey homeward to habitual self," "The goal of consciousness," and a reference to a loss of "freedom" indicate the general direction of the journey, as does the imagery of jewels in the center of the earth, like the "orbed diamond" whose illumination proceeds from a hard center. In proportion as the subjective consciousness is enclosed in itself, the object shuts itself up too and withdraws from human approach. The traditional symbol of this descent down the chain of being is metamorphosis, the stories of how female spirits (usually) fled from the passion of male gods and became enclosed in vegetable or animal forms. The poets of metamorphosis, Ovid and Apuleius, were favorites of Keats, and *Endymion* is intensely Ovidian, a revival not only of Spenser but of the Elizabethan Ovidian mythological poem, of which Drayton's *Endimion and Phoebe,* Shakespeare's *Venus and Adonis,* and Lodge's *Glaucus and Scilla* are examples. Whatever Keats' knowledge of Elizabethan poetry, all these stories are incorporated into *Endymion,* along with the story of Alpheus and Arethusa referred to above, which haunts Milton's *Lycidas* and *Arcades.* This separation of subject and object by metamorphosis was apparently the sequel of the conflict portrayed in *Hyperion,* which refers to

> *that second war*
> *Not long delay'd, that scar'd the younger Gods*
> *To hide themselves in forms of beast and bird.*

In Apuleius the changing of Lucius into an ass is a progressive degradation against which the lovely story of Cupid and Psyche floats up in the opposite direction, a particular favorite of Keats because it is late enough to be a myth created rather than believed, as myths for a Romantic poet essentially are. In Ovid, as in later writers, the central figure symbolizing metamorphosis as degeneration is the enchantress Circe, and Circe's connection with the story of Glaucus and Scylla is the reason why she is the presiding deity of Endymion's lowest world, the hell under the sea, where we might have expected rather the *diva triformis* herself in her infernal aspect of Hecate.

Just as the great Spenserian image of the Gardens of Adonis is at the center of the earthly and sexual world, so the Bower of Bliss, which also has marine associations in Spenser, is at the center of the water-world. The words "bower" and "bliss" occur in lines 418 and 427 of Book III. We are introduced to it, however, at a time when the delusory feeling of bliss has vanished and nothing but the sense of frustration and impotence remains. Keats' attitude to this world is not moral, like Spenser's: it is rather, however unpoetical the word may sound, epistemological. It is the world in which the separation of the conscious subject from everything it wants and loves is at its greatest, another version of the world of the bound Prometheus.

Even in the world of earth above, the love of Venus for

Adonis is already much more possessive than the love of Phoebe for Endymion, much more that of a Blakean "female will" who keeps the lover bound to a cycle of possession and loss. But Glaucus turns from his loved Scylla to Circe, a Jungian "terrible mother" who puts him into a "specious heaven" where he is a pure subjective consciousness. Like Milton's Satan after he separates himself from the community of God, Glaucus finds the new feeling of individuality exhilarating at first:

> *To interknit*
> *One's senses with so dense a breathing stuff*
> *Might seem a work of pain; so not enough*
> *Can I admire how crystal-smooth it felt,*
> *And buoyant round my limbs. At first I dwelt*
> *Whole days and days in sheer astonishment;*
> *Forgetful utterly of self-intent.*

But of course it quickly becomes, as with Satan, an imprisonment which reduces him to the narrowest of all prisons, the one he carries around with him as his own subjectivity. In this state of impotence he resembles Eliot's aged fisher king or Blake's Albion sleeping on the Couch of Death in Atlantis under the sea. The "fabric crystalline" in which Glaucus finds the dead Scylla suggests, like the "orbed diamond" of the previous book, a world which is visible but not approachable. Its poetic relatives include the crystal cabinet of Blake's poem in which the narrator struggles unsuccessfully to reach an "inmost Form," and the self-enclosed world of the unproductive and narcissistic beautiful youth of Shakespeare's sonnets, a "liquid prisoner pent in walls of glass."

The dead and shipwrecked lovers in the world of Circe's malignity remind us of the traditional Courtly Love convention, the cruel mistress gloating over her collection of slain lovers. Several times in Keats this nadir of human reality is presented as a world of ghosts frozen in a wintry world of death, an impotent shadowy Hades where "men sit and hear each other groan." Closest to the Courtly Love convention, of course, are the victims whom La Belle Dame Sans Merci has in "thrall" in a barren landscape of late autumn and withered sedge. There are also the "benightmared" and palsy-ridden creatures left behind by the escaping lovers in the bitter chill of *The Eve of St. Agnes*, including the Bedesman who remains "aye unsought for" in spite of all his prayers. A similar group appears to be clustering in *The Eve of St. Mark*. During the illness which forcibly separated him from Fanny Brawne, Keats felt that he himself had fallen into a world which he describes as

> *that most hateful land,*
> *Dungeoner of my friends, that wicked strand*
> *Where they were wreck'd and live a wrecked life.*

In general, the ghost or subjective shadow symbolizes this nadir-world, like the ghost of Lorenzo in *Isabella* whose murder has isolated him from humanity. Like all hells, it is not a world of death but of life in death, where the repose of death is unattainable.

Endymion's descent into the world of the "arbitrary queen of sense" is a somewhat rarefied allegory of an attitude to life in general which is much more clearly expressed in the letters. We notice how often Keats uses the word "identity" to describe men of action, those who exhibit strong personalities, drive their wills aggressively toward a visible goal, make up their minds and know where they are going. Poets, on the other hand, show something of the apparent weakness of those who, like pregnant mothers, have to bring something else to birth. Compared with the decisive man, the poet has no identity. His mind is not a fortress: he does not exclude enough. He is a thoroughfare for thoughts, ideas, and images; his capabilities are negative; his aim is less to do things than to let things happen. Endymion, too, says, very late in the poem:

> *What is this soul then? Whence*
> *Came it? It does not seem my own, and I*
> *Have no self-passion or identity.*

Saturn uses the word in a similar sense in *Hyperion*. Of course the decisive temperament may be found in creative people too: for Keats it certainly is in Byron, and there is a touch of it in the "egotistical sublime" of Wordsworth. The purest creative temperaments, however, notably Shakespeare, show least admixture of it.

The point is that there are two kinds of identity. They might be distinguished as *identity-as* and *identity-with,* and they represent respectively the two poles of Endymion's cosmos, the worlds of Circe and of Phoebe. Both kinds begin as consciousness or self-awareness, but one develops a hostile and the other a sympathetic relation to its surroundings. The decisive and aggressive temperament identifies himself as himself: his attitude is subjective, and he confronts an objective world set over against him. He usually does not realize that to the extent that he does so he loses his freedom and becomes a puppet of circumstance, for the subject confronts everything else, and, as the scroll that Glaucus obtains in Book III says, no one can devise a total opposition. Bonaparte, says Keats, was "led on by circumstance," in contrast to, for example, the Apollo of *Hyperion,* who says "knowledge enormous makes a God of me." The world of Circe is very hard on poets and lovers, but, though described in *Endymion* only in connection with them, it is also, in its larger context, the world of action and history.

This is the reason for the passages at the openings of Books II and III, which express respectively a preference for the heroes and heroines of literature over those of history, and for the spirits and gods of the imagination over the more socially accepted creatures who "lord it o'er their fellow-men." Poets and lovers create a society precisely the opposite of that of the decisive or domineering one, by identifying themselves with what they make or love. Both kinds of identity are ways of actualizing the unborn dream that is a part of everyone's mind. In the eyes of the world, the decisive person is the one who has outgrown the dream, and the creative or loving temperament the one that is still preoccupied with it. But the popular view is entirely wrong. The decisive person has merely congealed his dream into the more obsessive dream of subjective aggressiveness. Even when his "total opposition" fails and he is caught up into the externalized machinery of the objective world, his life does not cease to be a continuous somnambulism. It is the poet who understands the contrast between the creator and the dreamer. He does not awaken *from* his dream into a different world: he awakens the dream *into* his world, and releases it from its subjective prison.

This is what, on a larger scale, Endymion is doing for Glaucus, in an episode which resembles *The Tempest* crossed with a more primitive version of the *Tempest* story like the St. George myth. The arrival of Endymion from "over" the sea rejuvenates Glaucus, as his previous arrival on earth had revived Adonis, and the two begin to transform a shipwrecked society into a reintegrated one. The scroll they find informs them that they have to learn magic, like Prospero, and this magic is an art of releasing the "symbol-essences" of nature, delivering the spirits in the prisons of subject and object alike. There are also echoes of Hercules releasing Theseus in the lower world, and a good deal of imagery suggesting a version of the Theseus story in which all the previous sacrifices to Minos were delivered from the labyrinth. Echoes of the Christian Harrowing of Hell are less explicit. References to Arion in Book II and to Amphion, who appears to be assimilated to Arion, in Book III, and images of whales and dolphins, suggest the stories of Jonah and other voyagers to the viscera of leviathan. The dolphin, however, is traditionally the image of salvation from the water, and reminds us rather of Lycidas, who visited the bottom of the monstrous world but became a protecting genius of the shore and also a saint in heaven. Lycidas makes a remarkable reappearance in the lively little poem *Staffa,* one of the figures in the more Shelleyan cosmos that Keats began to develop after *Endymion,* in which renewed powers rise from below. During his descent Endymion had feared the total loss of his identity, and that he would suffer the traditional *sparagmos* fate of the god in the underworld and be torn "piece-meal." But instead it is the scroll that is torn up and that fertilizes the sunken world with a new life. The student of Romantic poetry should compare the image of the torn-up fertilizing scroll with the almost identical image in the speech of Orc in Blake's *America,* Plate 8.

The anabasis, or return to the upper states, has all the expected images of rebirth. We have Atlantis, the rainbow following the deluge, the reappearance of the sea-born Venus and the description of Neptune's throne as "emerald," which indicates a reunion of the sphere of water with that of the green earth. The hymn to Bacchus in Book IV, sung by the Indian maid, balances the hymn to Pan in Book I, but is a product, not simply of a state of innocence, but of a new energy that has returned to that world from experience. Endymion then takes to the air, and seems ready for his final ascent to the fire-world of the gods where Phoebe is. But overtones of Icarus and Bellerophon in the imagery warn us that all is not plain flying, and Endymion receives an abrupt check. He attempts a renewed pastoral life of the "Come live with me and be my love" type with his sister and the Indian maid, attempting to consolidate his gains and stay where he is, like Peter on the Mount of Transfiguration. It seems a sensible enough solution: it is clear that the four levels of the poem's cosmos are not a Platonic ladder, as Platonism is generally understood. It would be inconsistent with everything we know of Keats to assume that we ascend from the body into a higher world of the soul, abandoning the sexual basis of Eros, a basis which is also the matrix of all one's love and compassion for society. The only real Phoebe, on Keats' own postulates, would be an incarnate Phoebe, identical with the Indian maid. In Eliot's *Burnt Norton,* the "still point of the turning world" is a middle point identical both with the zenith of the vision of correspondence preceding it, and the vision of death under the yew-tree following it. Similarly, as truth and beauty are the same thing, the goal of the quest for beauty above and the goal of the quest for truth below would be the same point, and that point in turn identical with the worlds of Peona and the Indian maid in the middle.

The trouble is that Endymion's quest cannot be completed by an act of will. That was why the Courtly Love tradition, although it demanded the most strenuous efforts from the poet-lover, still made his ultimate success depend on the grace of his lady. Hence Endymion has to wait until he is "spiritualized" by an "unlooked-for change," at which point Phoebe, like Ligeia in Poe, takes over the Indian maid, and carries Endymion off to her own world. The world of this final assumption is still continuous with the physical and sexual world, but has transformed it in a metamorphosis which goes in the opposite direction from those celebrated by Ovid. The conclusion repeats an earlier theme in the fourth book. Endymion had previously found himself, just after his abortive flight, in the cave of Quietude, a cave of dreams like the Cave of Nymphs in the Odyssey from whence Ulysses returned home, a cave which also can be entered only involuntarily:

> *Enter none*
> *Who strive therefore: on the sudden it is won.*

The fully awakened vision of the poet, which includes truth or knowledge as well as beauty, depends, like the dream, on something beyond the conscious will, and the unlooked-for change at the end resolves the theme of "sleep and poetry" on which so much of *Endymion* turns. As Keats says in the letters: "The difference of high Sensations with and without knowledge appears to me this—in the latter case we are falling continually ten thousand fathoms deep and being blown up again without wings and with all [the] horror of a bare shouldered creature—in the former case, our shoulders are fledge, and we go thro' the same air and space without fear." The reference to Milton's Satan indicates that "knowledge," the element of truth which is part of beauty, makes the difference between sleep and poetry, dream and vision, chaos and creation.

An extraordinary number of fascinating mythical themes are touched on, explicitly and implicitly, in the fourth book of *Endymion*. Coming so late in the poem, they seem almost to suggest the need of a fresh start, and in fact there are signs of impatience and of a desire to begin again with the story of Apollo. Different as *Endymion* is from *The Prelude,* it is equally a poem about the growth of the poet's mind. The process of growth is presented through myth and archetype, and consequently has an impersonal and universalizing quality about it: it deals with *the* poet rather than, like *The Prelude,* with *a* poet. But the direction of the theme, and its personal reference to Keats, are both unmistakable:

> *There came a dream, showing how a young man,*
> *Ere a lean bat could plump its wintery skin,*
> *Would at high Jove's empyreal footstool win*
> *An immortality, and how espouse*
> *Jove's daughter, and be reckon'd of his house.*

What we have now to try to determine is what the relation of *Endymion* is to Keats' whole poetic vision. That is, what kind of poetry results from Endymion's experience, or, thinking of him in his final role as a god, from his inspiration?

The fourth book, along with the end of the third, is the part of *Endymion* that incorporates the pre-Romantic structure of myth, derived mainly from Spenser, into a Romantic cosmos. The nadir of this cosmos is the world normally symbolized in Keats, as in Beddoes, by ghosts or a paralyzed life in death. Blake calls it a world of "spectres," which includes both the people who live egocentric and jealous lives, the strong identities of Keats' letters, and the kind of abstract and generalized views of the world that such minds produce. The word "spectre" indicates a state where neither the subject nor the object is real: the real objective world is a world in itself, hidden behind the things we see and know, and our real selves are hidden behind our subjective egos. The poet can escape from this spectral world by his power of being able to articulate the language of "symbol-essences," a language which exists only through human creation, but which expresses the identity of the real subject and the real object. In Keats, as in Shakespeare and Shelley, this poetic power is symbolized by the magician who can command the spirits of the elements. The next step takes us into the world of the awakened imagination, where we pass beyond the elemental spirits to become united with the gods. This last stage of Endymion's pilgrimage is illustrated by the divine figures with which *Hyperion* and the great odes are so largely concerned.

Scylla, the beloved of Glaucus who is killed by Circe and brought to life again by this liberating magic, repre-sents the theme of the deliverance of the bride from im-prisonment in the lower world, which we meet so often in myth, from Proserpine to Beddoes' Sibylla. The theme of the failure of ascent is included in the fourth book of *En-dymion,* as we saw, and the most famous myth of such a fail-ure is the story of Orpheus and Eurydice. Keats returns to this aspect of his mythology in *Lamia,* a story which is pa-thetic rather than cautionary. But, of course, the major attempt to rewrite the anabasis of *Endymion* in terms of a different mythology is *Hyperion,* the theme of which is announced in *Endymion* itself.

Hyperion is Miltonic in its structure as *Endymion* is Spenserian. The fallen Titans, however, have not, like the devils in Milton, fallen outside the earth into a hell far be-low it: they are at the bottom of the ladder of identity, like the sea-world of Circe. They are gods of power who are now imprisoned, traditionally under volcanoes, actu-ally in the objectivity of nature. Hyperion, still undeposed, corresponds to the Father-God of Milton who is still pre-siding over his court in heaven although all real authority has been transferred to the Son. Out of this chaos of impotent power emerges Apollo, a Logos-figure who is both divine and human, and has achieved the poet's awareness of identity with his world. Probably a confrontation like the Son-Father confrontation of Demogorgon and Jupiter in Shelley, though in a very different context, would have come next, a struggle for the sun rather than the ocean.

The poetic universe of *Hyperion* is less traditional and more typically Romantic than the universe of *Endymion*. Keats had really two structural problems to solve for a complete *Hyperion*. One was the adapting of the old Miltonic up-and-down universe to a Romantic in-and-out one, where the presence of God, or what corresponds to God, is identified with the creative power in the poet's mind. The other was the adapting of the old spatial chain-of-being conception to a temporal one. For *Hyperion* also has a "historical" or "evolutionary" scheme, with one power succeeding another in time, which looks forward to a later phase of Romanticism, like that represented by Victor Hugo's *Légende des Siècles*. *Hyperion* begins, as all good epics should, in the middle. To solve the first problem the poet would need to work backward to the beginning in the poet's mind, as *The Fall of Hyperion* attempts to do; to solve the second he would need to go on with the story, in a narrative that would have taken him at least through the "second war" of metamorphosis.

It is clear from what we have said that one essential function of poetry, for Keats, is to help us move upward on Keats' version of the chain of being, toward an identity-with, or communion. The poetry that brings to birth the unborn vision of beauty, we said, is the opposite in theme of the poetry of metamorphosis, or the separating of subject and object, commemorated in Ovid and Apuleius, which is based on an alienation or fall archetype. We should not read the great odes, for example, as subjective contemplations of objects, which is the exact opposite of what they were designed to be. They are rather a recovery, by poetry, of the myth formerly projected as the worship of a god or numinous presence. In Christianity this act of worship is expressed in a symbolic act of communion, in the response of faith to a revelation symbolized by a divine Word, and in the forming of a church, or community of response. The Romantic counterparts of these would be, respectively, communion, or the identity of the poet and his theme which the poem itself articulates; communication, or the reader's understanding of the poem; and community, or the forming of a society of readers, or a literary tradition.

If I say "this pencil is green," I am making a statement about a sensation of my own, identifying the pencil with my own experience, that I cannot directly share with others. What makes it a statement of fact, or enables it to pass for one, is a verbal consensus: other people agree when I say it is green, though for all I know they may be seeing what I would call red. Thus communication is a by-product of communion, the verbalizing of the identity of one's inner life. Communication in its turn is the focus of community. As long as everyone agrees when I say this pencil is green, the possibility of their seeing what to me is red is one I can afford to ignore. And however trivial a statement about the color of a pencil may be, it is obvious that the verbal consensus which makes statements of fact possible is the basis of human culture. A statement of imagination is more flexible than a statement of fact, but the same three principles are involved. (The argument from here on has a few parallels with Heidegger's essays on Hölderlin, where three similar principles are described as world, language, and history.)

The poem, then, begins in the poet's experience of communion, or identity-with. This seems to be a private and subjective communion in which only the poet is involved, and so in one context it is. But the language of poetry is not a subjective language, nor is it objective like descriptive language, even when it uses the same words. It is the magical or spell-binding language of symbol-essences, the voice of the world where the mind behind the subject and the world behind the objects are united, where nature and personality are at one, as they formerly were in the sea-gods and sky-gods of ancient mythologies. We began this chapter by saying that in the Romantic period poetry becomes, not a substitute for or another form of religion, but, increasingly, the medium for understanding religion, as the sense of reality in religion slowly shifts over from the doctrinal and conceptual to the imaginative and mythical. Hence the analogies we have mentioned between Romantic poetry, as exemplified by both the theory and the practice of Keats and Shelley, and the Christian religion of their cultural milieu, go quite a long way. In religion, communion takes place within the body of a divine man who is also a liberating and creative Word, and whose home is Paradise. In these poets, the divine man is not the poet, but Man, the universal human mind of Shelley's Prometheus; the liberating Word is the voice of the imagination which speaks through poetry, and its task is to awaken the vision of the beauty of the uncreated world we have in ourselves, so that, like Adam who really was in Paradise, we awake to find the dream true.

The great odes, with their heavily brocaded texture and their sense of utter absorption in meditation, are the finest poems of communion, in the Romantic context, that the Romantic movement achieved. Like the great twentieth-century poems of meditation, Eliot's *Quartets,* they do not deal directly with the world of ordinary experience or with the demonic world. These worlds are there by implication, but in a context where their reality becomes unreal, just as the subway passengers in *Burnt Norton,* though their prototypes are in contemporary London, are present only as shadows in a fantastic Hades. Whenever the demonic world appears in Keats, in the terrible clarity of *La Belle Dame Sans Merci,* in the tragedy of Isabella, whose basilpot is a parody of the one-pointed contemplation of the odes, in *Lamia,* it is seen, like the foul monsters in Spenser's fairyland, from within the charmed circle of romance.

One obvious characteristic of communion-poetry is a tendency to synaesthetic imagery, as represented by the line in *Isabella:* "And taste the music of that vision pale." Such imagery includes the contact senses of taste and smell and feeling along with the more conventional images of sight and sound. The traditional symbols of communion are eating and drinking, and in communion poems we need draughts of vintage and the bursting of Joy's grape on the palate to complete the sense of identity-with. *The Fall of Hyperion,* though its argument leads up to a contrast between poet and dreamer, begins with a narcotic drink symbolizing the total immersion of the poet in his dreamworld. The display of food in *The Eve of St. Agnes* has not much to do with the plot, but has everything to do with the imagery and atmosphere. And just as all five senses have their place in a poetry of identity, so thought and reflection have a place equal to sensation. The famous remark "O for a life of sensations rather than of thoughts!" may be interpreted, using Eliot's categories, as an expression either of dissociated sensibility (O for a life of sensations instead of thoughts) or of unified sensibility (O for a life in which thoughts have the immediacy of sensations, instead of a life in which sensations are as unsubstantial as thoughts). The latter is the only possible meaning consistent with the odes, which identify truth with beauty as well as Grecian urns with the poet and his reader. The theme of sexual fulfillment is touched very lightly, but the odes are sufficiently about love to make it clear that what they celebrate includes what Blake would call an improvement of sensual enjoyment.

Unified sensibility of this sort also demands a catharsis of moods, a raising of emotions which frees one from their domination. Moods are like colors: all real experience is a blend of them, and to see life from within a single mood is a deliberately summoned up illusion, like putting on colored spectacles. Such an illusion is an entirely valid form of poetic experience, and there is no reason why a poet should not reduce his world, if he so wishes, to a green thought in a green shade. Milton's *L'Allegro* and *Il Penseroso* are an extraordinary *tour de force* of mood-poetry, each projecting an entire life through one of the two major and dominating moods, the gay and the grave. The eighteenth-century librettist who arranged these poems for Handel is said to have added a third section of his own, *Il Moderato,* depicting a properly balanced state of mind in the middle. We may perhaps take this as a symbol of everything that Keats disliked about the eighteenth century, and attacked in *Sleep and Poetry.* For Keats, joy and sorrow can only unite at the point of the greatest intensity of both, not in a lukewarm mediocrity halfway between them. This union is already present in the hymn to Bacchus in the fourth book of *Endymion,* which is enclosed in a song to sorrow, and it expands in the later work, where "Welcome Joy and welcome Sorrow" is a constant motif and where the identity of delight and melancholy, of joy and frustration, of escape and annihilation, of the *allegro* and *penseroso* moods everywhere, is constantly present.

But while joy and sorrow are different aspects of the same thing, beauty and ugliness are not. The identification of beauty and truth means that ultimately the conception of beauty would have to embrace the ironic vision as well as the romantic one, applying as much to Swift as to Keats. But in Keats' practice, as in general usage, the vision of beauty is a vision of loveliness, of the attractive world, the unborn Paradise. We noticed that the sinister and tragic in Keats are seen within the conventions of romance, which means that they are often seen as incomplete forms of the vision of beauty. Lamia, for instance, as previously suggested, is in some respects almost a Eurydice figure: perhaps if Lycius had not made two mistakes, one of listening to a Platonist who preferred thoughts to sensations, the other of letting in the public too soon, he might have gone all the way from Circe's world to Phoebe's, taking Lamia with him. The poetry of Keats as we have it is set against the world of experience, as something which is in that world but not of it. We see this particularly in Keats' style. The odes in particular depend on magic spells and charms, on the marking off of special holy places and the building of private temples in the mind, on escape from noise and vulgarity, on a watchword of *favete linguis* and on an intensely hieratic rather than a demotic consciousness. The style of such poetry has to be a rhetorical *tour de force,* kept up to a uniform level. Either we surrender to its spell or we leave the poem alone, and even if we do surrender to it, the tiniest variation in the mood would disturb us.

Such a style was not Keats' own ideal: his ideal was that of a completely flexible style, a style with the dramatic versatility of Shakespeare's. The hieratic or uniform style of *Hyperion* is associated by Keats, not strictly with Milton, but with Milton's influence on him. The revisions in *The Fall of Hyperion,* so far as style and diction are concerned, seem to have as their general aim the moving away from the homogeneity of *Hyperion* toward a more relaxed tone, one which suggests a story being told, as well as less striving for the invariably impressive rhetoric of deity. Keats associates this more flexible style not only with Shakespeare but with Chatterton, to whom he dedicated *Endymion*. Evidently he felt that the archaism of Chatterton could be the basis of a more concrete and specific style, capable of the familiar as well as the impressive, than the archaism of Milton with its more Latin bias. What we may feel to be the uncertainties of taste in *Endymion,* such as the clanging rhymes, are also part of an attempt to develop a style without levels, which can encompass the sublime and the familiar at once. The same ambition drove Keats later in his career into what have seemed to some of his readers very inappropriate experiments, such as the meandering shaggy-dog narrative of *The Cap and Bells.* His well-known advice to Shelley to "load every rift with ore" came at a time when he himself, stylistically speaking, had made several experiments with a much looser and more Shelleyan—even, in *The Cap and Bells,* Byronic—texture.

The state of identity-with is not merely a creative state; it is also a moral state corresponding to the older state of innocence which traditionally has been associated with the child. The sense that the child in particular responds to his surroundings to the point of identifying with them is central to Blake's *Songs of Innocence* and to Wordsworth, and is still there in Whitman's *There Was a Child Went Forth*. In Keats too there is a delightfully childlike quality in such expressions of identity as this from his letters: "if a Sparrow come before my Window I take part in its existence and pick about the Gravel." Such a state is innocent in the sense that sympathy, compassion, the ability to feel and participate in the moods of others, are natural by-products of it. The deep introversion of childhood remains at the heart of every vision of innocence, however, that does not expand into and incorporate a vision of experience. The poet is still in Endymion's second world, still identifying himself with his own creations, still trying to break out of the circle of Narcissus. We are not speaking of Keats here, but of a danger in this situation that Keats himself recognized.

Keats leaves us in no doubt that he wanted to develop further in the direction of a poetry of *concern*, a poetry that would incorporate the ironic vision and the state of experience and would meet Moneta's demand to recognize the reality of misery as well as the reality of beauty. For there is also a poetry of identity-*from*, a detaching vision of an absurd or anguished world, and Keats, no less than Shelley, was aware of the revolutionary social impact of poetry and of its role in helping to realize liberty:

> *there ever rolls*
> *A vast idea before me, and I glean*
> *Therefrom my liberty; thence too I've seen*
> *The end and aim of Poesy.*

Like Shelley, too, he thought of the poet's creation, which ultimately is a renewed human society, as greater than *the* creation, in the sense of an objective world which is largely a projection of our own cowardice or laziness. At any rate he speaks of the universe as containing "materials to form greater things [than] our Creator himself made," his meaning here being clearly more serious than his tone. In the few years he had, Keats constructed the two inner parts of his temple: the outer court of a poetry of experience had yet to come. The inference seems to be that Keats was a minor poet who would have become a major one if he had had a few more years of life and health. This seems very reasonable, except that every reader of Keats knows that it is wrong, and that his existing work has to be discussed in very different terms.

Keats, unlike Shelley, has no specific philosophical or religious affinities, but the ideas that come tumbling out of his letters are all the more endlessly suggestive. We have stressed the significance of the fact that we cannot read the great odes, in particular, as subjective contemplations of objects. The mind that contemplates, the poet with his negative capability, is the focus of a universal human mind, like Wordsworth's "motion and a spirit" with which the poet identifies himself. What is contemplated is a deity, or, like the Grecian urn, an emblem of a divine or paradisal existence. But the divine existence is not a substantial god, or rather, for Keats, goddess: the goddess is created by the poetic imagination, the agent of the creative human mind, which according to the Romantic myth is the real divine presence involved. We move into a sphere of being where the difference between art and nature, between the creature and the object, has ceased to exist. The music of the spheres and the poetry of man are the same thing, as Mnemosyne implies when she says to Apollo:

> *Thou hast dream'd of me; and awaking up*
> *Didst find a lyre all golden by thy side,*
> *Whose strings touch'd by thy fingers, all the vast*
> *Unwearied ear of the whole universe*
> *Listen'd in pain and pleasure at the birth*
> *Of such new tuneful wonder.*

Keats could get little help here either from a Christian monotheism or a Greek polytheism. For analogies to the kind of assumptions underlying his poetry we have to turn to Oriental religions, and when Keats in his letters says that "any one grand and spiritual passage serves [man]

as a starting-post towards all 'the two-and-thirty palaces,'"
the Oriental sound of the last phrase is significant. There
are types of lyrics in Chinese and Japanese literatures which
seem to be doing something deceptively simple, merely observing or recording a scene in nature. There is a famous
Japanese haiku, for example, which says in effect, in seven-
teen syllables, only "Frog; pool; splash." But such poems
do not really present the seeing of objects by subjects: the
poet's mind surrounds and contains what he describes, and
as his mind, according to the principles of most of the
philosophies and religions contemporary with such poetry,
is united to a universal mind in which all things are, he is
presenting a scene of nature in its proper context, where it
is both what the poet creates and what is really there.

The traditional term for the appearance of a divine presence in human life is epiphany, a term used in Christianity
for certain appearances of Christ, in particular to the Magi.
Joyce uses the word as a critical term in *Stephen Hero,* and
appears to have adopted it because of his full agreement
with the Romantic tendency to associate all manifestations
of divinity with the creative spirit of man. But Joyce seems
to have thought of the basis of the epiphany, in its literary
context, as an actual event, brought into contact with the
creative imagination, but untouched by it, so that it
preserves the sense of something contained by the imagination and yet actual in its own terms. As Stevens says, one is
more apt to confide in what has no concealed creator.
Wordsworth was the great pioneer, almost the discoverer,
of epiphany in this sense, as something observed but not
essentially altered by the imagination, which yet has a crucial significance for that imagination. Such poems as *Simon
Lee* are based on epiphanies in Joyce's usual sense of actual
(or, at least, readily credible) incidents, and *The Prelude*
is in the same sense an epiphanic sequence, a series of in-

cidents in the poet's life which by their arrangement take the form of an imaginative quest. The more recent cults of "found objects" in the visual arts, of "happenings" in the dramatic ones, and of chance progressions in music, testify to the continued vitality of the association between the random and the oracular.

Joyce and Wordsworth are mainly concerned with the kind of poetry of experience that Keats did not develop. Keats' odes are epiphanic in a narrower and more traditional sense. They are not concerned with objects or experiences found at random, but with icons or presences which have been at once invoked and evoked by a magical spell, and held as a focus of meditation. The contrast in itself is obvious but has important implications.

Another striking and powerful idea that peeps out of the letters and a few phrases in the poetry is also Oriental in most of its developments—an idea of interpenetration. "Every point of thought is the center of an intellectual world," Keats says. Every soul is at once the center and the circumference of the universe, hence the society the poet is trying to help form is an interpenetrating society, with the macrocosm present in each microcosm: "They interassimulate," as he says in an inspired portmanteau word. In such a world no one could be objective to anyone else. "Man should not dispute or assert but whisper results to his neighbour and thus by every germ of spirit sucking the sap from mould ethereal every human might become great, and Humanity; instead of being a wide heath of Furze and Briars with here and there a remote Oak or Pine, would become a grand democracy of Forest Trees!" For such a society the outer court of experience would not need to exist, and even poetry would recover its original power of silence, retreating from communication to pure communion and becoming the "spirit ditties of no tone." The home of such poetry could only be in a renewed or regenerate Nature, of the kind indicated by the Zen master who speaks of the beauty of cherry-trees when a disciple asks him how to attain Buddhahood, or by Wordsworth when he finds "the types and symbols of eternity" in an ordinary traveler's journey, or by Shelley in his enigmatic symbolism about a nature restored to health with the liberation of man. In such a nature everything would be epiphanic, with the world present in a grain of sand and heaven in a wild flower.

Shelley also uses the word "interpenetrate" in *The Defence of Poetry* in a way which indicates that the conception is in his thought too, but it seems even more central to Keats, and better illustrated by Keats' practice. This seems strange at first, for Keats is not an apocalyptic seer in the way that Shelley, Blake, Wordsworth at times, and many Oriental poets are. He is closer to Eliot in stressing the effort of meditation, and the discipline necessary to quiet the soul and the restlessness of an activistic conscience. "The soul," he says, "is a world of itself and has enough to do in its own home." Keats is a poet of the *temenos,* the marked-off holy place, the magic circle of *The Eve of St. Agnes* with the lovers inside and hostility and bitter cold outside. His paradise is not a timeless and spaceless Eden, but a Castle of Alma surrounded by malignant ghosts.

Keats' three great pre-Romantic predecessors had all looked at the paradisal vision in the context of the fall: for them it was something man has lost, and cannot regain through his own efforts. His efforts are essential, but they are moral efforts: man cannot create or recreate paradise, though God may put him back into it after the moral quest has been completed. Dante's Eden is explicitly on top of the mountain of purgatory, but Spenser's Faerie and Milton's "Paradise within thee, happier far," also, we saw, belong to a Purgatorio rather than a Paradiso. Similarly,

Keats speaks in his *Epistle to Reynolds* of the imagination being lost in a "Purgatory blind," and the vale of soul-making spoken of in the letters is also a purgatorial conception. The moral earnestness of Keats drew him closer to these predecessors than to any direct transcendence of experience. The kind of nature-mysticism we have just associated with Wordsworth, Shelley, and Zen Buddhism seems to be talking about a nature which, like the myth of Paradise itself, is more of a *picture* of nature than existential nature, something to be contemplated but not lived in. It may be true as far as it goes, but if we compare it with the ferocity and horror that nature, including human nature, actually exhibits, once we enter into its processes, our "natural piety" would soon make Dr. Pangloss look like a realist by comparison. In the soul-making passage Keats says: "But in truth I do not at all believe in this sort of perfectibility—the nature of the world will not admit of it —the inhabitants of the world will correspond to itself. Let the fish Philosophise the ice away from the Rivers in winter time and they shall be at continual play in the tepid delight of Summer." In the *Epistle to Reynolds,* just mentioned, he goes on to speak of "an eternal fierce destruction" as the essence of his vision of nature.

The traditional solution of the problem of attaining an innocent vision in the midst of a ferocious nature is, of course, that the real end of the innocent vision is not in this life at all, but in what Keats calls this life's "spiritual repetition" in another world. The soul, Keats says, achieves its identity through the interaction of three principles, a mind or intelligence, a "heart," and the "World or Elemental space." It is this last in particular that is the purgatorial element. The interpenetrating world, just described, is clearly a world without space, and once the soul's identity has been achieved, the "World or Elemental space" would disappear. In the world of immortality, Keats says, "there will be no space," and nothing left of what Blake calls the cloven fiction of subjects and objects. This brings us to the great vision which is at the heart of *Endymion,* the upper world that Endymion finally attains, described in a passage which, as we know from a letter to his publisher Taylor, Keats regarded as crucial:

> *Wherein lies happiness? In that which becks*
> *Our ready minds to fellowship divine,*
> *A fellowship with essence; till we shine,*
> *Full alchemiz'd, and free of space. Behold*
> *The clear religion of heaven!*

In its context, this spaceless world is, by definition, the world of a future life, as distinct from the present life where world and space are the same thing. It is also the lost paradise or innocent vision of a previous life: we notice how the word "forlorn," with its overtones of something glimpsed but out of reach, echoes in the *Ode to a Nightingale*. Similarly, the vision of being without becoming suggested by the Grecian urn is the kind of paradox that we are forced to use in searching for some analogy in language to describe a higher kind of existence. At the same time, Keats' conception of poetry as the voice of an interpenetrating world is Romantic in the sense that it regards human creative power as the only thing which gives us any clue to what another dimension of life may be like. Eliot, more distrustful of what the Romantic movement brought, tells us that it is the function of art to bring us to a state of serenity and then to leave us, "As Virgil left Dante, to proceed toward a region where that guide can avail us no farther." Keats sees in poetry a power that can bring us into an interpenetrating world in which the word "farther" ceases to mean anything. Perhaps his intuition is not only profounder and saner than Eliot's, but is one more relevant to a civilization like ours.

The Romantic movement began, in English literature, with the sense that the individual subject was no longer a self-explanatory unit of experience. Philosophers and theologians had always known this, as a matter of theory, but now it became a question of practical life as well. For Wordsworth, the individual subject found its identity in a larger unity gained through an imaginative contact with a "nature" standing outside and apart from human society. Wordsworth regarded his account of this sense of larger identity as consistent with its more traditional religious formulations, but in traditional religious terms his own expression of it was vague and loose, as it had to be and as it should have been. Coleridge was more belligerently Christian in insisting that the primary imagination was an existence repeating the infinite "I am" of God, and in feeling that every argument he advanced on the point was one in the eye for atheism, skepticism, and "psilanthropism." In Burke we see, much more clearly than in Coleridge, that this new sense of identity does have a real enemy. Burke identifies the enemy with the Jacobinism of the French Revolution. Burke's view of the French Revolution itself, however, is not very rewarding: what is important is his prophetic vision of the kind of society that we now call totalitarian, where the sense of identity is restricted to society, where the sense of the continuity of tradition is annihilated, and where the general will of society is unconditioned by any reference to a goal beyond the immediate objects of those in power.

The Romantic poets, especially Keats, preserve the feeling that at the heart of the best and fullest life is something anti-social, or more accurately something beyond society which is still essential to human identity. It is not important what we call this, or rather, it is important that different people should call it different things. Today, technology has created for us a society in which each man is made aware of an entire world of experience, interpenetrating with the awareness of all his neighbours. Human nature being what it is, its first response to this situation is to create out of it a hell of unparalleled hysteria. We can no longer live in the relatively comfortable and quiet hell of *The Waste Land,* where "each man fixed his eyes before his feet," but are plunged into the whirlwind of the mob itself, where there is no rest and no escape. When we search for the inner resources that the same mind can draw on in trying to deal with a *demonic* interpenetrating world, poetry takes on a new importance, especially the poetry that seems most directly opposed to it. Thus the Romantic vision of Keats itself acquires, in the course of time, the militant and crusading quality of a poetry of experience.

This is merely a special case of the general principle that no poetry of high intensity covers a part only of the imaginative world: it covers its entire range, by implication at least. We saw how the impetus of Keats' imagination was carrying him in the direction of a poetry of concern and compassion, of songs of experience in which the connection of sleep, with its wish-fulfillment dreams, and poetry had finally been broken off. But in the course of time his written poetry becomes also, for us, what his unwritten poetry would have been. When the poet has done all he can in communion and communication, the responsibility for forming the third element of literature, the community of response, rests on us. In the *Bhagavad-gita* Arjuna, fighting his kinsmen on a battlefield, wanted to escape from the fight to a world of greater reality. His charioteer, the god Krishna in disguise, convinced him that there was nowhere to go, and after that, Arjuna saw on the battlefield the epiphany of the universe in the body of Krishna. The song of the nightingale, the "cold Pastoral" of the Grecian urn, the magic casements in the castle of the soul that open to the warm love rising from the perilous seas seem to us, at first, images of a poetry of refuge, a dream of a lost Paradise. That is a possible but shallow response: the disciplined response understands that these poems are visions on and of the battlefield itself, not the subjective fantasies of retreat. Only a community which has disciplined itself to respond can even hear the voice of Keats' whispering democracy, the voice of a society which includes both nature and humanity, a being solidly rooted in a ground of being, and uniting death to life.

Notes

p. 8 "cult of a 'horned god.'" See Margaret Murray, *The Witch Cult in Western Europe* (1921).

p. 12 "Coleridge." In "On Poesy or Art": see *Biographia Literaria*, ed. Shawcross, II, 257–258.

p. 15 "social sciences." Cf. Elie Halévy, *The Growth of Philosophic Radicalism*, tr. Mary Morris (1928), ch. i.

p. 15 "pre-Romantic." This word in this book means the whole period from the beginning of the Christian era down to the latter part of the eighteenth century.

p. 22 *"Davidsbündler."* I take this term from Robert Schumann's piano music: cf. the *Davidsbündlertänze,* op. 6, and the conclusion of the *Carnival,* op. 9 ("Marche des Davidsbündler contre les Philistins").

p. 26 "popularity of Scott." For a violent and roughly contemporary reaction to this see George Borrow's *The Romany Rye* (1857), ch. vii of the Appendix.

p. 27 "mythical constructs." The influence of these has, paradoxically, popularized the notion that Romanticism has no consistent imaginative structure, but is only a chaotic period of subjectivity and relativism, at most a number of contradictory tendencies, following the dissolution of the great chain of being. It is hoped that the present book, along with some of those listed in the bibliography, will help the reader to put Humpty Dumpty together again by himself.

p. 43 "Praz's influential book." This is, of course, Mario Praz: *The Romantic Agony* (1933).

p. 48 "series of phases of myth." The scheme of the present book perhaps owes something to that of D. G. James: *The Romantic Comedy* (1948), though the differences in attitude are obvious.

p. 52 "instead of publishing it then." I am not suggesting that it was Beddoes' fault that his play was not published earlier, only that it is always unfortunate for literature not to have important works published in their primary chronological place. I think this principle applies also to the poetry of Hopkins.

p. 59 "It has been noticed." Edward E. Bostetter's *The Romantic Ventriloquists* (1963) deals with this feature of Romantic poetry, though it is not concerned with Beddoes.

p. 62 "Bagehot's . . . comments." "Wordsworth, Tennyson, and Browning; or, Pure, Ornate, and Grotesque Art in English Poetry" (1864).

p. 62 "Stevenson." "The Works of Edgar Allan Poe," *Essays and Reviews*.

p. 66 "like Goethe." I owe this view of Goethe to Barker Fairley: *Goethe's Faust: Six Essays* (1953).

p. 70 " 'world's sign is taken down.' " From Gosse: the Donner Variorum edition has another and much more verbose reading.

p. 72 "Demeter to her Proserpine." This remark, on reflection, seems pointless, except that it is true that Beddoes' world of the dead tends to become, like Shelley's world of immortality, an explicitly mythological world.

p. 84 "Kant's riddle." There seems in fact to be a definite influence from Kant on Beddoes: see H. W. Donner: *Thomas Lovell Beddoes* (1935), 213.

p. 91 "Berkeley." In the essay *On Life* (1815). For Godwin as a possible intermediate influence here see the edition of Godwin's *Political Justice* by F. E. L. Priestley (1946), iii, 109.

p. 98 " 'green world.' " *Prometheus Unbound,* III, iv, 39; *Endymion,* I, 16; *The Bride's Tragedy,* III, v, 8.

p. 100 " 'tyranny of Greece.' " E. M. Butler: *The Tyranny of Greece Over Germany . . .* (1935).

p. 102 "Christian Trinitarian myth." If this book had been a study of German Romanticism, the three poets chosen would (probably) have been Kleist, Heine, and Hölderlin. The substitution of Heine for Shelley would have made this part of the argument easier to follow, as Heine adopts the old Joachim of Floris conception of the dawn of a third age of the Spirit following after the ages of Father and Son. See the ballad "Tannenbaum, mit grünen Fingern" in *Die Harzreise* (1826). Similarly in Blake, the martyred Son-figure, Orc or Luvah, is the son, not of the Father-figure Urizen, but of the Spirit-figure Los.

p. 105 "books." In particular, Anders Nygren, *Agape and Eros,* tr. Philip S. Watson (1953), and *The Mind and Heart of Love,* by M. C. D'Arcy, S.J. (1945).

p. 132 "Byron." See Leslie Marchand: *Byron, A Biography* (1957), (II) 886.

p. 135 "Rilke." Letter to Ellen Delp, Oct. 27, 1925.

p. 150 "Heidegger's essays." Martin Heidegger: *Erläuterungen zu Hölderlins Dichtung* (1951). Two of Heidegger's Hölderlin essays are translated in *Existence and Being* (1949), ed. Werner Brock.

p. 158 "Stevens." "So-and-So Reclining on Her Couch," *Collected Poems* (1954), 296.

p. 162 "Eliot." "Poetry and Drama," *On Poetry and Poets* (1957), 87.

Bibliography

There are many bibliographies of Romanticism available, and the present one is simply a list of books which seem to me most helpful in studying the imagery, symbolism, and mythology of the English Romantic poets. For obvious reasons there is a strong bias in favor of recent books. No attempt has been made to list the standard biographical or historical studies.

Abrams, M. H. "The correspondent breeze: a Romantic metaphor," *Kenyon Review*, XIX (winter 1957), 113–130.

———. *The mirror and the lamp: Romantic theory and the critical tradition.* New York: Oxford University Press, 1953.

Baker, Carlos. *Shelley's major poetry: the fabric of a vision.* Princeton, N.J.: Princeton University Press, 1948.

Beer, John. *Coleridge the visionary.* London: Chatto & Windus, 1959.

Blackstone, Bernard. *The consecrated urn: an interpretation of Keats in terms of growth and form.* London and New York: Longmans, Green, 1959.

———. *The lost travellers: a romantic theme with variations.* London: Longmans, Green, 1962.

Bloom, Harold. "Afterword," in Mary Shelley, *Frankenstein* (New York: New American Library, 1965), pp. 212–223.

———. *Shelley's mythmaking.* New Haven, Conn.: Yale University Press, 1959.

———. *The visionary company: a reading of English Romantic poetry.* Garden City, N.Y.: Doubleday, 1961.

Bowra, C. M. *The Romantic imagination.* Cambridge, Mass.: Harvard University Press, 1949. (The Norton Lectures, 1948–1949.)

Bush, Douglas. *Mythology and the Romantic tradition in English poetry.* Cambridge, Mass.: Harvard University Press, 1937. (Harvard Studies in English, vol. 18.)

Evert, Walter. *Aesthetic and myth in the poetry of Keats.* Princeton, N.J.: Princeton University Press, 1965.

Fairchild, Hoxie Neale. *The noble savage: a study in Romantic naturalism.* New York: Columbia University Press, 1928.

Ferry, David. *The limits of mortality: an essay on Wordsworth's major poems.* Middletown, Conn.: Wesleyan University Press, 1959.

Ford, Newell F. *The prefigurative imagination of John Keats: a study of the beauty-truth identification and its implications.* Stanford, Calif.: Stanford University Press, 1957.

Frye, Northrop (ed.). *Romanticism reconsidered: selected papers from the English Institute.* New York: Columbia University Press, 1963.

Gittings, Robert. *John Keats: the living year, 21 September 1818 to 21 September 1819.* Melbourne: Heinemann, 1954.

Hartman, Geoffrey. *Wordsworth's poetry, 1787–1814.* New Haven, Conn.: Yale University Press, 1964.

Hilles, F. W., and Harold Bloom (eds.). *From sensibility to Romanticism: essays presented to Frederick A. Pottle.* New York: Oxford University Press, 1965. (Includes essays by Geoffrey Hartman, Kathleen Coburn, E. D. Hirsch, Earl R. Wasserman, Harold Bloom, and M. H. Abrams.)

Hirsch, E. D. *Wordsworth and Schelling: a typological study of Romanticism.* New Haven, Conn.: Yale University Press, 1960. (Yale Studies in English, vol. 145.)

Knight, G. W. *The starlit Dome: studies in the poetry of vision.* London: Oxford University Press, 1941.

Kroeber, Karl. *The artifice of reality: poetic style in Words-*

worth, Foscolo, Keats, and Leopardi. Madison, Wis.: University of Wisconsin Press, 1964.

————. *Romantic narrative art.* Madison, Wis.: University of Wisconsin Press, 1960.

Lindenberger, H. S. *On Wordsworth's Prelude.* Princeton, N.J.: Princeton University Press, 1963.

Lowes, John Livingston. *The road to Xanadu: a study in the ways of the imagination.* Boston, Mass.: Houghton Mifflin, 1927.

Marsh, Florence. *Wordsworth's imagery: a study in poetic vision.* New Haven, Conn.: Yale University Press, 1952.

Nethercot, Arthur H. *The road to Tryermaine: a study of the history, background, and purposes of Coleridge's "Christabel."* Chicago: University of Chicago Press, 1939.

Notcutt, H. C. *An interpretation of Keats's Endymion.* New York: Haskell House, 1964. (First published 1919.)

Perkins, David. *The quest for permanence: the symbolism of Wordsworth, Shelley, and Keats.* Cambridge, Mass.: Harvard University Press, 1959.

————. *Wordsworth and the poetry of sincerity.* Cambridge, Mass.: Belknap Press of Harvard University Press, 1964.

Rieger, James. *The mutiny within: the heresies of Percy Bysshe Shelley.* New York: G. Braziller, 1967.

Thorslev, Peter L. *The Byronic hero: types and prototypes.* Minneapolis: University of Minnesota Press, 1962.

Wasserman, Earl R. *The finer tone: Keats' major poems.* Baltimore: John Hopkins Press, 1953.

————. *The subtler language: critical readings of neoclassic and Romantic poems.* Baltimore: John Hopkins Press, 1959.

Wilson, Milton. *Shelley's later poetry: a study of his prophetic imagination.* New York: Columbia University Press, 1959.

Woodman, Ross G. *The apocalyptic vision in the poetry of Shelley.* Toronto: University of Toronto Press, 1964. (Univ. of Toronto, Dept. of English, Studies and Texts no. 12.)

Index

Actaeon, 134
Adam, 17, 18, 24, 128
Adonis, 136
agape, 20, 104, 105
Allston, Washington, 94
Alpheus and Arethusa, 137, 138
Amphion, 144
Anaximander, 77
Apuleius, 138, 139
Aquinas, St. Thomas, 5
Arion, 144
Aristophanes, *The Frogs*, 63
Aristotle, *Poetics*, 35, 68
Arnold, Matthew, 39
Atlantis, 111, 144
Augustine, St., 109
Austen, Jane, 45; *Love and Freindship*, 29

Bacon, Francis, 27
Bagehot, Walter, "Wordsworth, Tennyson, and Browning . . . ," 62, 168
Barham, Richard, *The Ingoldsby Legends*, 75
Baudelaire, Charles, 19, 44; *Correspondances*, 29-30
Beckett, Samuel, 63

Beddoes, Thomas Lovell, 12-13, 33-34, 48, 51-85, 116, 118-119, 147, 148, 168; *The Bride's Tragedy*, 51, 53-55, 57, 98, 169; *Death's Jest-Book*, 51-52, 56-67, 69; *The Last Man*, 67, 77; *The Second Brother*, 55-56, 76
Berkeley, George, Bishop, 91
Bhagavad-gita, 164
Bible, 5, 6, 17, 114; *see also* mythology, Biblical
Blake, William, 13-14, 22, 24, 36, 44, 70, 91, 107, 111, 113, 140, 147, 153, 169; *America*, 18, 144; *The Book of Thel*, 131, 133, 137; *Europe*, 13; *The Four Zoas*, 59; *Jerusalem*, 38; *Milton*, 38; *Songs of Innocence and Experience*, 33, 155
Bonaparte, 142
Borrow, George, *The Romany Rye*, 168
Bosch, Hieronymus, 61
Bostetter, Edward E., *The Romantic Ventriloquists*, 168
Brontë, Emily, *Wuthering Heights*, 31
Browne, Sir Thomas, 7, 21
Browning, Robert, 62, 118; *The Bishop Orders His Tomb*, 67

Bunyan, John, *The Holy War*, 30; *The Pilgrim's Progress*, 38
Burke, Edmund, 27, 163
Butler, E. M., *The Tyranny of Greece over Germany*, 169
Butler, Samuel, 53; *Erewhon*, 133
Byron, George Gordon, Lord, 18, 31, 36, 39, 60, 74, 142, 155, 169; *Cain*, 26, 31, 34; *Childe Harold*, 31, 41, 42, 59, 75; *The Corsair*, 74; *Don Juan*, 44, 59, 75; *Lara*, 31; *A Vision of Judgement*, 14, 31
Byronic fiction, 97
Byronic hero, 30-31, 41

Cain and Abel, 30, 31
Camus, Albert, *L'Etranger*, 44
Carlyle, Thomas, 27, 39-40, 85; *Sartor Resartus*, 39
Carroll, Lewis, *Alice in Wonderland*, 132
Catullus, Attis Ode, 6
Cave of the Nymphs, 146
Chatterton, Thomas, 155
Chaucer, Geoffrey, 24; *The Pardoner's Tale*, 72
Chekhov, Anton, 64
Christ, 7-8, 13, 17, 31, 33, 34, 105-106, 108, 123
Christianity, 6-8, 10, 13, 16, 100, 104-105, 122-123, 150-151, 158, 163
chronos, 109
Circe, 139, 140
Coleridge, S. T., 12, 18, 20, 27, 94, 163, 167; *Kubla Khan*, 33, 80; *The Rime of the Ancient Mariner*, 16, 18, 41, 63
confessional form, 41-42
Constant, Benjamin, *Adolphe*, 43
courtly love, 42, 43, 131, 140-141, 145
Crabbe, George, 37
Cronos, 109

Cupid, 136-137, 139
Cybele, 6, 136

danse macabre, 56, 65
Dante, 7, 114-115, 123; *Commedia*, 5, 129-130; *Convivio*, 13; *Inferno*, 134; *Paradiso*, 7, 24; *Purgatorio*, 117, 118, 133; *Vita Nuova*, 104
D'Arcy, M. C., S.J., *The Mind and Heart of Love*, 169
Darwin, Charles, 62, 64
De Quincey, Thomas, 15; *Confessions of an English Opium-Eater*, 42; *The English Mail-Coach*, 93
Diana, 133, 135, 136, 137
Dickens, Charles, 64; *The Old Curiosity Shop*, 62
Dickinson, Emily, 113
Dionysus, 7-8, 16, 20, 99-100
Donne, John, 67
Donner, H. W., *Thomas Lovell Beddoes*, 169
Drayton, Michael, *Endimion and Phoebe*, 138
dream, 128

Eden, 17, 19, 24, 32, 126, 130, 133
Eliot, T. S., 15, 27, 60, 67-68, 117, 152, 160, 162, 169; *Ash Wednesday*, 117; *Burnt Norton*, 122, 133, 135-136, 145, 152; *The Cocktail Party*, 117; *The Dry Salvages*, 85; *East Coker*, 60; *Four Quartets*, 151; *Gerontion*, 67; *Marina*, 117; *The Waste Land*, 19, 63, 67-68, 117, 140, 164
elpis, 105
epiphany, 158-159
Eros, 8, 9, 16, 20, 52, 113, 114, 123-124, 137, 145
eros, 20, 104, 105

Esau, 30, 31, 97
Eurydice, 148, 154

Fairley, Barker, *Goethe's Faust,*
168
"fall," 17
Flaubert, Gustave, 44
Foscolo, Ugo, *Ultime Lettere di
Jacopo Ortis,* 43
Freud, Sigmund, 17, 32, 98, 123

Galileo, 11
George, St., 141
God, 7, 9, 10, 13, 14, 15, 17, 21,
23, 24, 25, 31, 36, 37, 47, 87-
88, 95-96, 101, 102, 149
Godwin, William, 169
Goethe, J. W. von, 15, 36, 66,
168; *Faust,* 14, 40, 103; *Wer-
ther,* 43
Golden Age, 19, 24
Gothic, 26, 29, 66, 69, 132

haiku, 158
Halévy, Elie, *The Growth of Phil-
osophical Radicalism,* 167
Handel, G. F., *L'Allegro ed Il
Penseroso,* 153
Hardy, Thomas, 11; *The Dynasts,*
25
harrowing of Hell, 144
Hazlitt, William, 23; *Liber Amo-
ris,* 43
Hegel, G. W. F., 112
Heidegger, Martin, on Hölderlin,
150, 169
Heine, Heinrich, 169
Hercules, 144
Hölderlin, J. C. F., 59, 150, 169
Holy Spirit, 30
Homer, Odyssey, 146
Hooker, Richard, 14
Hopkins, G. M., 168
Horace, 6

Hugo, Victor, 5; *La Légende des
Siècles,* 149
Huxley, Aldous, *Point Counter-
point,* 132

Ibsen, Henrik, *When We Dead
Awaken,* 32
imagination, 20, 23, 128
incest, 113
Ionesco, Eugene, 64
Ishmael, 30, 31, 97
Israel, 17

James, D. G., *The Romantic Com-
edy,* 168
Joachim of Floris, 169
Johnson, Samuel, *Rasselas,* 133
Jonah, 144
Joyce, James, 3, 15, 158, 159; *A
Portrait of the Artist,* 120;
Stephen Hero, 158
Judaism, 6
Jung, C. G., 65

Kant, Immanuel, 84, 111, 169
Keats, John, 36, 52, 115; *La
Belle Dame Sans Merci,* 141,
152; *The Cap and Bells,* 155;
Endymion, 18-19, 25, 46, 49,
98, 125-165, 169; *Epistle to
Reynolds,* 161; *The Eve of St.
Agnes,* 141, 152, 160; *The Eve
of St. Mark,* 141; *The Fall of
Hyperion,* 38, 59, 139, 142,
148-149, 154-155; *Isabella,* 141,
152; *Lamia,* 148, 152, 154;
odes, 148, 149-153, 157, 159,
165; *Ode on a Grecian Urn,*
127, 157, 162; *Ode to a Nightingale,* 162; *Otho the Great,* 59;
Sleep and Poetry, 153; *Staffa,*
144
Kierkegaard, Søren, 32
Kleist, Heinrich von, 59, 169

Laforgue, Jules, 25
law, 9, 14
Lawrence, D. H., 15, 16, 20, 132
Lodge, Thomas, *Glaucus and Scilla,* 138
Lucifer, 31, 103; *see also* Satan
Lucretius, *De Rerum Natura,* 6
Lytton, E. Bulwer, *A Strange Story,* 29

Maeterlinck, Maurice, 66
Malthus, T. R., 121
Marchand, Leslie, *Byron, A Biography,* 169
Marlowe, Christopher, *The Jew of Malta,* 60
Medusa, 113
metamorphosis, 138, 149
Milton, John, 5, 15, 22, 129, 138, 146, 154-155; *L'Allegro* and *Il Penseroso,* 153; *Il Penseroso,* 101; *Comus,* 103; *Lycidas,* 138, 144; *Nativity Ode,* 11, 120; *Paradise Lost,* 18, 34, 44, 102, 106, 129, 133, 140, 148, 160; *Paradise Regained,* 108
Morris, William, 36-37, 66
Murray, Margaret, *The Witch Cult in Western Europe,* 167
myth, 4-5
mythology, Biblical, 17, 78, 114
mythology, Christian, 6, 7, 8, 10, 16, 169
mythology, Classical, 6, 9, 16, 34, 100
mythology, matriarchal, 6, 7, 8, 18
mythology, medieval, 7, 16
mythology, pre-Romantic, 19, 20, 21, 23-24, 32
mythology, Renaissance, 9

Napoleon, 142
Narcissus, 78-79, 140, 156
Newton, Isaac, 11

Nietzsche, Friedrich, 7, 73; *Also Sprach Zarathustra,* 32
Noah's wife, 8
noble savage, 18
Novalis, 20
Nygren, Anders, *Agape and Eros,* 169

Oedipus, 103
Oriental affinities in Keats, 157-161
Orpheus, 148
Ossian, 35
Ovid, *Metamorphoses,* 6, 138, 139, 146

Paley, William, 121
Pan, 133-135
Pascal, Blaise, 47
pastoral, 9
Peacock, Thomas Love, *The Four Ages of Poetry,* 121
Plato, 104, 105, 112, 123; *Phaedo,* 118; *Timaeus,* 6
Poe, Edgar Allan, 26; *Hop-Frog,* 72-73; *King Pest,* 62; *Ligeia,* 145
Pound, Ezra, 27
Praz, Mario, *The Romantic Agony,* 43, 168
Proserpine, 148
Proust, Marcel, *A la Recherche du Temps Perdu,* 15, 43

Radcliffe, Mrs. Ann, 29
Rembrandt, 94
Ricardo, David, 15
Rilke, Rainer Maria, 16, 135, 169
Rimbaud, Arthur, *Une Saison en Enfer,* 34-35
Romantic irony, 43
Romanticism, 3-5, 15, 16, 168
Rousseau, Jean-Jacques, 18, 27-28, 44, 121; *Confessions,* 41-42

Sade, Marquis de, 43-44
Samuel, 80
Satan, 8, 96, 102, 106-107, 129;
  see also Lucifer
Schiller, Friedrich, 36
Schopenhauer, Arthur, 32, 53
Schumann, Robert, *Davidsbündlertänze*, 22, 167
science, 10, 11
Scott, Sir Walter, 26-27, 29, 36-37,
  168; *The Lay of the Last Min-
  strel*, 27, 31
Seneca, 64-65; *Thyestes*, 61
Shakespeare, William, 23, 45-46,
  57, 60, 66, 68, 70, 97-100, 142,
  154; *Antony and Cleopatra*, 56,
  99; *As You Like It*, 45; *Cymbe-
  line*, 66; *Hamlet*, 40-41, 56, 60;
  Macbeth, 60, 68; *The Merchant
  of Venice*, 45; *A Midsummer
  Night's Dream*, 35, 39, 45, 98,
  136-137; *Romeo and Juliet*,
  131; *Sonnets*, 140; *The Tempest*, 99, 113, 141, 148; *Titus
  Andronicus*, 61; *Venus and
  Adonis*, 138
Shaw, G. B., 6
Shelley, Percy Bysshe, 14, 18, 20,
  21, 26, 34, 67, 76, 101, 132,
  148, 151, 155, 156, 157, 160;
  Adonais, 134; *Alastor*, 41, 113;
  The Cenci, 44, 105, 111; *The
  Cloud*, 94; *The Defence of
  Poetry*, 96, 107, 120, 122, 160;
  Epipsychidion, 104, 113; *Essay
  on Christianity*, 121; *On a Future State*, 117; *Hellas*, 41, 101,
  119, 120, 122, 123; *Hymn to
  Intellectual Beauty*, 104; *Julian
  and Maddalo*, 113; *On Life*, 91,
  107, 169; *Mont Blanc*, 115; *Ode
  to Heaven*, 114; *Ode to the
  West Wind*, 30; *Prince Athanase*, 101; *Prometheus Unbound*, 14, 38, 46, 48-49, 87-
  124, 149, 169; *Queen Mab*, 13,
  41, 89-91, 95-96, 99, 101, 102,
  106, 110; *The Revolt of Islam*,
  88-89, 109, 110, 117, 119; *The
  Sensitive Plant*, 118; *Song to
  the Men of England*, 119; *The
  Triumph of Life*, 120, 121; *The
  Witch of Atlas*, 92
Shelley, Mary, 119; *Frankenstein*,
  44-45, 107
Silenus, 100
sister-bride, 18, 113
sky-gods, 14
Spenser, Edmund, 147; *The Faerie
  Queene*, 25, 30, 129, 133, 136,
  139, 152, 160; *The Shepheards
  Calender*, 134
Stevens, Wallace, 158, 169
Stevenson, R. L., 62, 168
Strindberg, August, 16, 64, 66;
  The Dream Play, 68; *The
  Great Highway*, 32
Synge, J. M., *The Playboy of the
  Western World*, 75

Tasso, 107
Teilhard de Chardin, Pierre, 15
Tennyson, Alfred Lord, 26, 52;
  Ulysses, 67
Thanatos, 52
Theseus, 144
Tolkien, J. R. R., *The Lord of
  the Rings*, 108
Tourneur, Cyril, *The Revenger's
  Tragedy*, 57
Traherne, Thomas, 32
Turner, J. M. W., 94

Vaughan, Henry, 32
Verhaeren, Emile, 19
Vico, Giovanni Battista, 14
Virgil, Fourth Eclogue, 114

Wagner, Richard, *The Ring of the
  Nibelungs*, 108
wanderer, 38

Wandering Jew, 41, 83, 123

Webster, John, *The Duchess of Malfi*, 57, 66-67

Whitman, Walt, *There Was a Child Went Forth*, 155

witchcraft, 8

Witch of Endor, 80

Wordsworth, William, 12, 18, 19, 29, 30, 32, 43, 53, 84, 92, 97, 115, 142, 155, 157, 159, 160, 163; *The Excursion*, 38-39; *Ode on Intimations of Immor-* *tality*, 17, 32; *The Prelude*, 19, 20, 37, 39, 59, 147, 158-159; *Resolution and Independence*, 39; *Simon Lee*, 158

Yeats, W. B., 15, 16, 20, 25, 27, 64, 66, 101, 103; *The Tower*, 117

Zen Buddhism, 160, 161